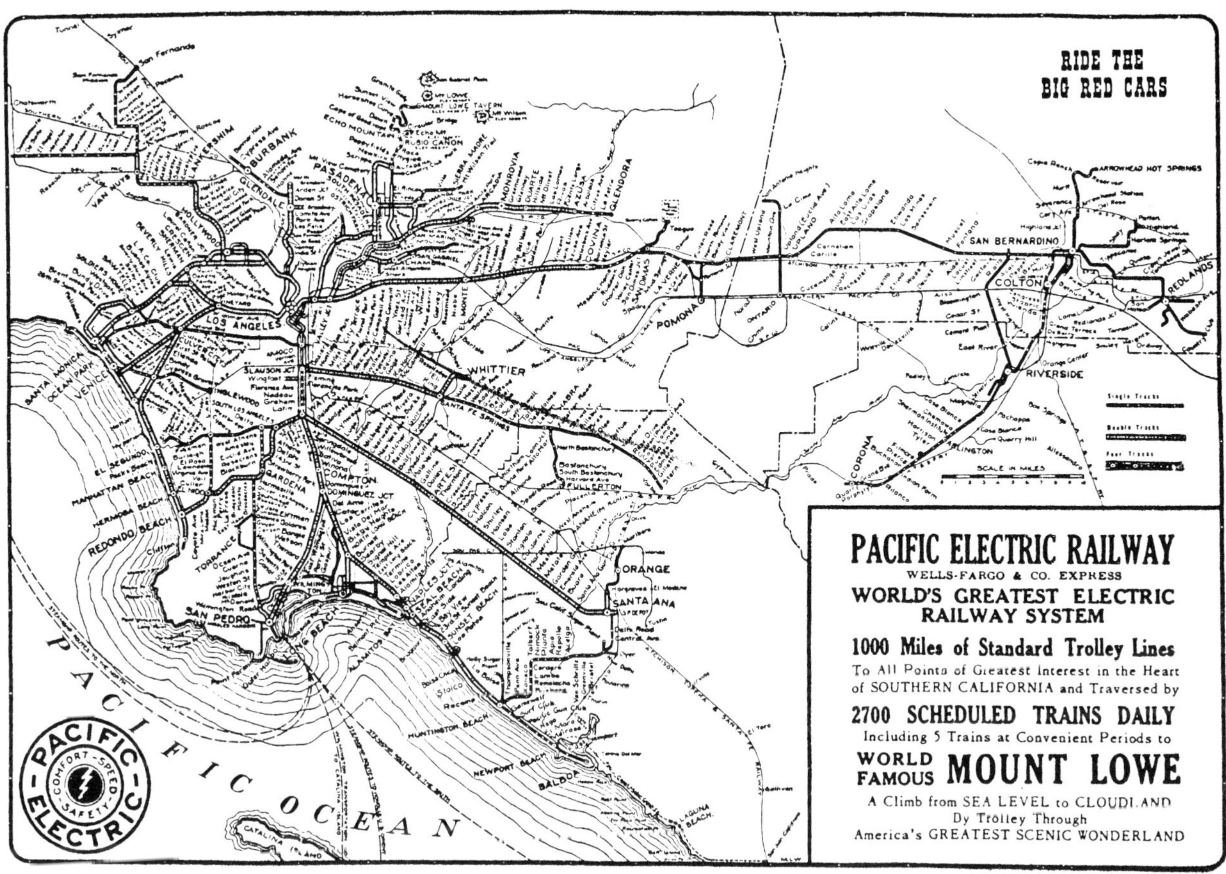

The network of Pacific Electric lines as operations reached a peak during the mid-1920's is depicted in this map. Trolley routes stretched over Los Angeles, Orange, San Bernardino, and Riverside Counties. The tracks skirted the seashore and climbed into the mountains, linking cities and farmlands.

HENRY HUNTINGTON and the PACIFIC ELECTRIC

SPENCER CRUMP

•

TRANS-ANGLO BOOKS
GLENDALE, CALIFORNIA

BOOK DESIGN: HANK JOHNSTON

BOOK COVER: Combination baggage-passenger car 498 heads a Catalina Special train, seen here at Willowbrook (between Watts and Compton) in 1957, en route from Los Angeles to the docks at Wilmington. Upon arrival, passengers will board the "Great White Steamship" for a voyage to Catalina Island.
Allan W. Styffe

BACK COVER: Henry Huntington's name lives on in many Southern California locations. In the upper photo, it is the evening rush hour on June 21, 1950. Here at Sierra Vista, where the Alhambra-Temple City line curves off from the four-track Northern District main line, the Watts-Sierra Vista local (center) is at the end of its run. In the foreground, a two-car train of "Twelves," P.E.'s finest interurbans, speeds towards Pasadena via the Short Line, while, in the left background, another train of "Twelves" heads for Los Angeles. On either side of the tracks, Huntington Drive carries commuters homeward, albeit in private automobiles. In the lower photo, circa 1956, two trains wait for passengers at the Sixth and Main Station of the Pacific Electric. Opened in 1905, the structure, known as the Huntington Building, was the first tall office building in a city worried about earthquakes. Although the tracks have all been long since removed, the building remains in use today. **Above, Fred Matthews; below, Jim Walker**

HENRY HUNTINGTON AND THE
PACIFIC ELECTRIC
A Pictorial Album

FOURTH EDITION, REVISED 1987

Library of Congress Catalog Card Number: 78-67843

ISBN: 0-87046-048-X

FRONTISPIECE: Henry E. Huntington, founder of the Pacific Electric, enjoys a leisurely moment at his palatial home in San Marino. (Security Pacific National Bank)

Printed and Bound in the United States of America

Published by TRANS-ANGLO BOOKS
a division of INTERURBAN PRESS
P.O. Box 6444 • Glendale, California 91205

DEDICATION

To the Memory

Of My Grand Parents:

Margaret Payne Person
John Wesley Person

Introduction

The Pacific Electric, once the biggest and most efficient electric railroad in the world, served Southern California commuters and helped develop growth patterns for half a century.

This book is a brief history of that colorful railroad, with an emphasis on the pictorial aspects.

The Pacific Electric interurbans, affectionately called "Big Red Cars" by passengers and system employees, were as familiar to Southern California commuters as the smogless skies and waxy green orange groves which once made the area beautiful.

The Big Red Cars sped from San Fernando to Redlands, and from the San Gabriel and San Bernardino Mountains to tracks stretching along the Pacific from Santa Monica to Newport Beach. From 1902 until their final departure in 1961, the trolleys not only made commuting a pleasure but during their peak of operations also provided colorful sightseeing trips.

The founder of the Pacific Electric was Henry E. Huntington, nephew of Collis P. Huntington, a co-founder of the Central Pacific. Beginning in the early twentieth century, Henry Huntington's electric car lines stretched from Los Angeles out to what were then farming areas. The frequent trolley service produced the impetus for the growth of cities.

As efficient as the system was, it couldn't compete with automobiles. Roads cut through right-of-ways and autos filled city streets carrying tracks; interurbans were forced to travel more slowly. Automobiles and buses were more mobile than interurbans, and economic problems developed for the P. E. when passenger patronage fell.

Even though automobiles eventually antiquated the Pacific Electric, the interurban system could have been salvaged by modernizing right-of-ways and using fast electric cars. A $20 million improvement program in 1950 might have provided a model rapid transit system; by the 1970's, with many tracks gone, the price tag of such a network would be nearly $2 *billion*.

Rapid transit, once highly regarded by investors, apparently no longer can be operated even by governments without huge deficits. The day undoubtedly will come when, with crowded cities and packed streets, rapid transit will be financed entirely by the government and rides will be free.

My interest in the Pacific Electric developed when I was a youngster. My family didn't have a car, but my mother, Mrs. Jessie Person Crump, and my grandparents, John and Margaret Person, took me on sightseeing trips via the Pacific Electric and gave me many happy memories.

While the P. E. system is now gone, its fame lingers on — among the people who rode the

The Pacific Electric's Big Red Cars are perpetuated in museums and models. The author shows a P. E. scale model to his mother, Mrs. Jessie Person Crump, and his children, John Spencer and Victoria Elizabeth Margaret. (Photograph by Lawrence Saavedra)

Big Red Cars and those of new generations who have only heard about them.

When I took my children, John Spencer and Victoria Elizabeth Margaret — who were born after the Big Red Cars quit their routes — to see and ride the P. E. cars preserved at the Orange Empire Railway Museum at Perris, California, I found them fascinated by the trolleys and interurban era.

The youngsters, along with adults who never saw the Red Cars, asked questions regarding exactly where the trolleys ran and how frequently they operated. This book therefore includes a digest of the major P. E. routes — including exactly *where* the tracks were laid so that you can retrace the lines. I also have included typical schedules and running times on routes.

I believe the text and photos will help to refresh the memories of those who rode the Big Red Cars who also will help those who did not visualize the system.

Interest in the Big Red Cars continues to grow, of course, and I am accumulating more illustrations and facts on the system which I hope to include in a new book.

Again, I emphasize that this book is a brief pictorial history of the Pacific Electric. For those who are interested in more details, I suggest my book, *Ride the Big Red Cars: How Trolleys Helped Build Southern California.*

Ride the Big Red Cars presents dramatic details concerning the Pacific Electric and those associated with it. The volume offers more details concerning Henry Huntington, discusses the P. E.'s relationship with specific cities, and traces the rise and fall of the interurban empire. The book is profusely illustrated with photographs that do not appear in this volume.

For assistance in producing *Henry Huntington and the Pacific Electric,* I thank many individuals and organizations. Rather than attempting to name them in this introduction and risking an omission, they are credited with the photographs they made available.

SUGGESTED READING

Cleland, Robert Glass, *California in Our Time;* New York: 1947. A history of the state's development after 1900.

Crump, Spencer, *Ride the Big Red Cars: How Trolleys Helped Build Southern California (Third Edition, Revised);* Los Angeles: 1970. A detailed and illustrated history of the Pacific Electric and its predecessors.

Hilton, George W., and John F. Due, *The Electric Interurban Railways in America;* Stanford: 1960. A history of trolley systems throughout the nation.

Johnston, Hank, *The Railroad That Lighted Southern California (Second Edition, Revised);* Los Angeles: 1966. The story of Henry E. Huntington's Big Creek hydroelectric project.

Nadeau, Remi, *City-Makers: The Story of Southern California's First Boom, 1868-76 (Second Edition, Revised);* Los Angeles: 1966. The history of Los Angeles' early growth.

TABLE OF CONTENTS

Cable cars served riders prior to coming of the trolleys in the 1890's. This car, operating on South Broadway in 1889, belonged to the Boyle Heights & Downey Ave. Cable Car Railway. (Hugh Tolford Collection)

The Trolleys Come to Los Angeles

The Big Red Cars of the Pacific Electric were once as familiar to Southern Californians as the freeways of today. The P. E. could proudly and honestly boast that it was the world's biggest interurban system. At its peak in 1926, the company operated 1,164 miles of track stretching from the San Fernando Valley to Redlands and from the seashore into the San Gabriel and San Bernardino mountains.

For more than a half century, the Big Red Cars carried Southern Californians from their suburban homes to work in the cities and on pleasure trips to the beaches and mountains.

In 1911, it took just forty-one minutes for P. E. "flyers" to carry commuters from Ocean Boulevard and Pine Avenue in Long Beach to Sixth and Main Streets in the heart of Los Angeles' business section. A Big Red Car could go in thirty-five minutes from there to Colorado and Fair Oaks in downtown Pasadena.

Passengers could ride from Los Angeles to downtown Santa Monica or Whittier in fifty minutes, even during the hours with the heaviest traffic. "Rush" hour travel times from Los Angeles were Redondo Beach, fifty-seven minutes; Santa Ana, seventy-eight minutes; Glendale, thirty-five minutes, and Glendora, sixty-eight minutes.

Other 1911 Big Red Car commuter schedules from Los Angeles included Covina, an hour;

Horse-drawn streetcars also served before coming of the trolleys. This is Lyon Street, looking south from First Street, at Santa Ana in about 1889. (Security Pacific National Bank Historical Collection)

Huntington Park, sixteen minutes; San Pedro, forty-five minutes; Huntington Beach and Newport, sixty-three and seventy-six minutes respectively; La Habra, forty-eight minutes, and Beverly Hills, thirty-two minutes.

Riders on these and other Pacific Electric routes had freedom from traffic worries without asking. As a bonus, passengers could enjoy card tournaments or discussion groups with commuters who rode the same cars daily.

The electric interurban was the descendant of the horse and cable streetcars built during the second half of the nineteenth century. A number of inventors experimented with electric cars, but the man who developed the system most widely used in America was Frank J. Sprague, a graduate of the United States Naval Academy and an assistant to Thomas Edison when the latter was perfecting the electric light. His first installation was on the Union Passenger Railway at Richmond, Virginia, where trolleys began operation in 1888. The electric railroad immediately was declared a success. Entrepreneurs throughout America began building trolley systems in cities and villages.

The "trolley" name was applied to the cars because they obtained their electrical power from a pole that rode beneath a overhead wire. The small trucks that rolled against the wire were called "trollers," a term that was corrupted to "trolleys."

The trolleys which ran on their own right-of-ways between cities were called "interurbans," while those that operated on tracks laid on public roads, usually in cities, were called "streetcars."

Horseless carriages were a distinct luxury in this era; not only were they expensive, but there were few roads graded well enough for a pleasant trip over a distance as short as even fifteen miles. The investors who financed construction of interurban lines and the electrification of horse streetcar systems envisioned bonanzas.

Of the hundreds of trolley systems constructed during the quarter of a century following Frank Sprague's unveiling of his invention, the Pacific Electric would become the nation's most famous — and probably most efficient. The P. E. itself was the product of merging numerous interurban companies.

Southern California was ripe for electric railroads in the late nineteenth century. Cattle-raising and agriculture predominated; the 1890 census gave Los Angeles, the area's larglest city, only 50,395 residents. The coming of the transcontinental Southern Pacific and Santa Fe railroads produced booms in the 1870's and 1880's, but the cities founded during these decades remained little more than villages. Part of their problem was relative isolation from Los Angeles, the area's center of culture, commerce, and job opportunities. The railroads ran only limited daily passenger service between the villages and Los Angeles because the traffic hardly warranted frequent trains.

The electric interurban changed the picture. Every trolley was a train; its crew of a motor-

Giving horses or mules "free" rides down hill after they faithfully pulled streetcars on the upgrade was a feature of several lines in the 1880's. ABOVE: Animal-power gets a lift on the Euclid Avenue route of the Ontario and San Antonio Heights Railway. (Title Insurance and Trust Co.) BELOW: The driver stands by the animals on Monrovia's Myrtle and Ivy Avenues line. (Security Pacific National Bank)

This Cahuenga Valley Railroad cable car, pictured in the early 1890's when pulled by a small engine, served the area that became Hollywood. The P. E. took over its route. (Security Pacific National Bank)

man and a conductor made it more economical to operate than a steam train with more equipment requiring an engineer, fireman, conductor, and brakeman as its minimum personnel.

By the mid-1890's, trolley lines, many built from horse streetcar routes, criss-crossed Los Angeles. There were no interurban lines, but this minor deficiency soon was remedied by General Moses H. Sherman, a native of Vermont and once active in the Arizona territorial government, and his brother-in-law, Eli P. Clark, an Iowan who became a financier in Arizona. In 1890, the pair purchased Los Angeles' initial electric streetcar line. Buying other streetcar routes, they unified their holdings into the Los Angeles Consolidated Electric Railway.

Sherman and Clark then formed the Los Angeles and Pasadena Railway Company. Using portions of local lines between the two cities they forged the area's first interurban system. Ten trolleys dramatically opened the line on May 4, 1895, by speeding from Pasadena to Los Angeles.

The line was successful and the pair immediately began extending the electric railroad to Santa Monica, at the time the beach resort most favored by Los Angelenos. They followed the pattern that had been successful in building from Pasadena by using portions of smaller railroads. They also used land donated by property owners who reasoned that their adjoining holdings would be more valuable if served by an electric railroad providing more frequent service than on the existing Southern Pacific route.

The Sherman and Clark Pasadena and Pacific Railway Company line cut through the mustard fields that were to become Beverly Hills and Hollywood and came to its terminus on the ocean front at Santa Monica. The line opened, with much ceremony, on April 1, 1896.

Despite the success of the lines, Sherman and Clark couldn't raise cash to pay bondholders. They managed to retain ownership of the route from Los Angeles to Santa Monica, renaming it "Los Angeles and Pacific Railroad." But new owners took over their other trolley holdings. Chicago investors bought the route to Pasadena. A group of San Franciscans that included Henry E. Huntington purchased the Los Angeles Railway Company, successor to the Sherman and Clark Los Angeles Consolidated Electric Railway.

This acquisition marked the Los Angeles entry of Henry Huntington, the man who was to develop the Pacific Electric system.

An 1889 picture shows how the Los Angeles Cable Railway spanned the Los Angeles River to Downey Avenue. Electric trolleys, faster and more efficient, replaced cable cars. (Security Pacific National Bank)

The Man Who Built the P.E.

Henry Edwards Huntington can very well be said to have been born with a golden railroad spike in his mouth.

His uncle was Collis P. Huntington, aggressive member of "The Big Four" that built the Central Pacific and subsequently formed the Southern Pacific. Henry was born February 27, 1850, in Oneonta, New York. He worked briefly in his father's general store and in 1869, at the age of nineteen, left Oneonta to accept a job with his uncle. This path eventually led him to fame as a financier and patron of culture.

Collis, who had no children of his own, grew fond of his nephew, and Henry Huntington was regarded as the logical successor to the S. P. presidency. But when "C. P." died in 1900, financiers blocked Henry's ascension to the Southern Pacific throne. He subsequently sold the immense S. P. holdings left him by his uncle for $50 million. The buyer was E. H. Harriman, who was in the process of building a rail empire.

Henry Huntington evidently nurtured a great desire to follow in his uncle's footsteps. He was not one to be easily deterred. He proceeded to launch his Pacific Electric empire with rails competing in Southern California with the Southern Pacific. He also divorced his wife and married his uncle's widow, Arabella (who was thirty-two years younger than

Collis but only three younger than Henry Huntington).

Henry Huntington was enthusiastic over the potential of developing Southern California and, unlike most electric railroad builders of the day, was well capitalized. After buying the Los Angeles street railway interests formerly held by Sherman and Clark, he acquired the line from Los Angeles to Pasadena from the investors who had bought it.

Henry Huntington then began building a Los Angeles area network of electric railroads, much to the annoyance of steam railroad officials in general and E. H. Harriman in particular. Newspapers of the day ran dramatic discussions of Huntington's plans to extend his electric railroad system from San Diego to San Francisco via both coastal and inland routes. Much proposed trackage would duplicate Harriman's S. P. routes.

Many trolley systems were built, for economy reasons, with narrow gauge tracks and thus could not carry cars from steam railroads. By contrast, Huntington's electric railroads were standard gauge (4'8½") and could interchange with the transcontinental railroads. Trolley builders ordinarily cut costs by laying as much track as possible in streets, thus precluding the use of freight trains. Henry Huntington was wealthy enough to use private right-of-ways for the most part, thus permitting his electric railroads to do almost anything that a steam one could do.

His trolley system could menace the status quo of steam railroads in regard to passenger service as well as hauling freight.

Henry Huntington and a group of associates incorporated the Pacific Electric Railway Company on November 10, 1901, to carry out his program.

The first line built was to Long Beach, twenty miles from Los Angeles and then a village of approximately 2,200 residents. The line

Henry E. Huntington holds a brief business conference at the Santa Fe Station on Santa Fe Avenue between First and Second in Los Angeles (Los Angeles Times)

Henry Huntington posed for this picture in 1920 at his San Marino estate. RIGHT: Huntington's trolley empire stretched eastward to Redlands. Tracks and the overhead wire carrying power dominated the city's Orange Street in a photo made during the early 1900's. (Both photos: Security Pacific National Bank)

opened July 4, 1902, with the Red Cars bringing 30,000 visitors to the little town. Meanwhile, Huntington was standard-gauging and improving the route between Los Angeles and Pasadena, and building a line to Alhambra.

Huntington appointed Epes Randolph, a former S. P. executive, as vice president and general manager of the Pacific Electric. Randolph charted a vast trolley system with lines going in all directions from Los Angeles. The routes connected cities so directly that many of Southern California's first freeways paralleled them.

Travelers hailed Henry Huntington's trolleys. They preferred interurbans which, unlike the steam trains, ran frequently and could make quick stops and starts. Steam trains soon lost most of their local passenger business to the trolleys. Moreover, Huntington's standard gauge electric railroad system offered freight service with connections to transcontinental lines competing with the Southern Pacific. The Huntington-Harriman controversy was a story with daily developments.

The Southern Pacific had lost its battle to build a "monopoly" harbor at Santa Monica and a "free" port was being built at San Pedro. The S. P. hoped, nevertheless, to keep this harbor to itself as much as possible. Huntington, ordering crews to work one week-end, crossed the Southern Pacific right-of-way to reach the port with tracks before the company could obtain an injunction. His electric railroad tracks also were approaching potential commercial harbors at Newport, Anaheim Bay, Sunset Bay, and Long Beach.

The Southern Pacific fought back. One move was buying, in 1903, the substantial interest in the Pacific Electric held by Huntington associates.

Huntington was undaunted by having the S. P. as an unwelcome partner. He countered by forming the Los Angeles Inter-Urban Railway Company and the Pacific Electric Land Company. He personally bought virtually all of the stock in the two corporations and used them to continue building his trolley empire. Through these companies he eventually controlled lines to Huntington Beach and Newport, Santa Ana, San Pedro, La Habra, Covina, Monrovia, and Sierra Madre.

Incidentally, Huntington's interests were not confined to interurban systems. He also was building and buying "local" streetcar lines, regarded as potentially profitable in those days when few people owned horseless carriages.

In 1905, Huntington announced that he had acquired not only the Los Angeles and Redondo Railway, previously an independent electric line, but also the Redondo Land Company which owned most of the property at Redondo Beach. Not to be outdone, the Southern Pacific promptly bought a major interest in the Los Angeles and Pacific Railroad, the line built to Santa Monica by Moses Sherman and Eli Clark. This company competed with the Los Angeles and Redondo for traffic on Santa Monica Bay.

Laborers construct the P. E. line to Glendale in 1904. The system was built largely by Mexicans who were paid low wages and provided with inferior living quarters. (Security Pacific National Bank)

He also expanded his trolley empire by purchasing existing companies. Huntington bought the electric railroad connecting Los Angeles and Glendale. He made extensive acquisitions in the "Orange Empire" of Riverside and San Bernardino Counties by buying the Riverside and Arlington Railway Company, San Bernardino Valley Traction Company, San Bernardino Inter-Urban Railway Company, and the Redlands Central Railway Company.

Henry Huntington continued to compete with the Southern Pacific until 1908, when his interests began to turn from electric railroads and to other fields, including development of a

Streetcars typically dominated downtown streets from 1890 to 1940. ABOVE: A 1905 photo shows the trolley line on Third near "E" Street in San Bernardino, an area where Huntington was active. BELOW: A streetcar in Monrovia was decorated for a fete in the 1890's. (Both Pictures: Security Pacific National Bank)

magnificent estate at San Marino and expansion of his electric power holdings. In that year, he leased his electric railroad properties to the Pacific Electric, in which he shared ownership with the Southern Pacific. Two years later he sold his interurban holdings, including his share of the Pacific Electric, to the Southern Pacific.

The Southern Pacific operated these interurban properties as entities for two years. On September 1, 1911, it consolidated the companies into a new corporation, Pacific Electric Railway Company, and plans were made to apply red paint to all trolleys (most non-P. E. cars were green). Selection of the new company's name obviously gave tribute to Henry Huntington's Pacific Electric, whose Big Red Cars had grown famous in a decade.

Merged into the new Pacific Electric were the Los Angeles and Pacific, the Pacific Electric, Los Angeles Inter-Urban, the Los Angeles and Redondo, the San Bernardino Valley Traction, San Bernardino Inter-Urban, Redlands Central, and Riverside and Arlington railroad companies.

This consolidation later became known to railroaders and historians as "The Great Merger."

Automobile travel was still in its infancy and the Southern Pacific expected to reap bountiful profits from an electric railroad system serving a growing area. Optimistic over prospects of more electric railroad commuters, it extended the Covina P. E. line to Pomona, San Bernardino, Redlands, and Riverside, and completed direct connections between Riverside and San Bernardino. The Big Red Cars began service between Pomona and Los Angeles on September 1, 1912, and the line from Los Angeles to San Bernardino officially opened on July 11, 1914. There were subsequent extensions of the P. E. system, but the link between Los Angeles and the Orange Empire was the last big building program.

A Pacific Electric car on Colorado Street near Fair Oaks Avenue in Pasadena stops for passengers. The car was on the West Colorado Street-Orange Grove Avenue line in 1905. (Craig Rasmussen Collection)

Redlands was the most distant area from Los Angeles served by Huntington's trolleys. This photo, made in the early 1900's, shows a car on Orange Street, in Redlands' business section. (Redlands Daily Facts*)*

The Great Days of the Trolleys

The Big Red Cars helped bring immense growth to Southern California from their arrival in 1902 until well into the 1920's, when automobiles were commonplace. The population of Long Beach, first community touched by the magic of the Big Red Cars, grew from a village of 2,200 residents to a city of nearly 18,000 in less than a decade. Most of its new residents arrived on the P. E.

Other cities also grew when the Pacific Electric linked them to Los Angeles. Virtually all area real estate developments from 1900 to 1925 boasted they were conveniently situated near trolley tracks. Commuting by electric railroad was an accepted part of life in Southern California.

The biggest single land development tied to the Big Red Cars was the San Fernando Valley, connected to the Hollywood line by tracks through Cahuenga Pass. The valley's developers, well aware of the appeal of trolleys, made land available for the Pacific Electric right-of-way as part of their master plan.

Preoccupation over mechanical details of electric railroads frequently leads many students of the Pacific Electric to overlook the people who operated the system. Most of the P. E. tracks were laid by laborers imported from Mexico and initially housed in company camps. These men were poorly paid; in 1910, for example, the company gave $1.50 to $1.75 for a ten hour day, as compared to the $2.50

ABOVE: Laborers, many of whom were recruited in Mexico, build the Pacific Electric tracks on Holt Avenue in Pomona. The overhead wire already is up. (Pomona Public Library) BELOW: Trolleyman Dewey R. Tingler poses in his car on the Edendale Line during the early 1920's. (Jeannie Boggs Collection)

to $3.00 daily paid by other companies for similar labor. The fact that Mexico was in a political upheaval and wages there were low created the situation whereby the laborers were willing to work for such low pay. Conductors and motormen also received relatively low pay. In 1914, for example, they received twenty-five cents an hour as a starting wage and advanced to thirty cents an hour after five years. The low wages coupled with other job opportunities in a growing area made the P. E. labor turnover higher than on other trolley systems. Wages for track laborers and trolleymen gradually increased during the years. The rapid turnover then stopped, and many employees worked until retirement age.

One unusual facet of the Pacific Electric was its Mount Lowe line, climbing into the San Gabriel Mountains above Altadena. Unlike other routes, it was operated primarily for sightseers and vacationists. Built by Thaddeus S. C. Lowe, a balloonist for the Union forces during the Civil War, the line opened in 1893. The line's outstanding feature was a cable railroad carrying passengers approximately 1,500 feet from a pavilion in Rubio Canyon up a sixty per

Passengers prepare for the scenic ride in a cable car on the Mount Lowe incline railway, an unusual feature of the P. E. system. The cars left from Rubio Canyon, above Altadena. (Hank Johnston Collection)

This narrow gauge trolley rounds a curve in Las Flores Canyon en route from top of the cable incline to the Mount Lowe Tavern. (Craig Rasmussen Collection)

cent grade to Echo Mountain. From there, travelers rode narrow gauge (3'6") trolley cars around 127 curves and eighteen trestles to the base of Mount Lowe, at 5,000 feet above sea level. Here there were dining facilities as well as a hotel and cabins. Lowe lost control of the facility in 1896, and it became part of the Pacific Electric system in 1902. From Mount Lowe, visitors could look down, in those presmog days, on the Los Angeles area. Many days were so clear that Catalina Island, more than forty miles away, was visible.

The nineteen-mile trolley trip from Los Angeles to the pavilion in Rubio Canyon took approximately seventy-five minutes. The ascent via cable car to Echo Mountain covered just ten minutes, but it required a half hour for the 3.57-mile ride in a narrow gauge trolley with open sides around 127 curves and over eighteen trestles to the Alpine Tavern on Mount Lowe.

The narrow gauge ride was thrilling and the view from the trolleys was inspiring. Passengers never complained about the time required for the trip.

There were occasions when it snowed at the 5,000-foot level, and the mountain trolleys continued to operate. Children reared in the Los Angeles basin, where snow was an extreme rarity, then enjoyed a treat.

The tavern burned September 15, 1936, and in March, 1938, a cloudburst destroyed most of the mountain trolley system. The line never was rebuilt.

While the Pacific Electric concerned itself mainly with commuters and freight, it also catered to pleasure-seekers. It operated several "special" excursion trips for area residents and out-of-state visitors. Among these guided tours were the Balloon Route Trolley Trip, operated over a balloon-shaped route on the Los Angeles-Pacific system from Los Angeles to Santa Monica, Venice, Redondo Beach, and return. The Old Mission Trolley Trip took visitors to Mission San Gabriel and the Ostrich Farm in South Pasadena. The Triangle Trolley Trip went from Los Angeles to Santa Ana, Huntington Beach, Long Beach, San Pedro, and return. The Orange Empire Trolley Trip, launched after completion of the tracks to San Bernardino, went from Los Angeles to Riverside, Redlands, and San Bernardino.

Lower priced automobiles and better roads brought a discontinuation of most "special" trips during the 1920's. "Special" Pacific Electric trains continued to run to the Catalina Island ship terminal in Wilmington as well as to the Pasadena Tournament of Roses, the Los Angeles County Fair at Pomona, and the National Orange Show in San Bernardino.

The Pacific Electric hit its peak of operations during the 1920's. Interurbans rolled through Cahuenga Pass to the San Fernando Valley, sparsely settled with houses and chicken ranches and still awaiting the World War II boom that brought wholesale developments. The Big Red Cars, traveling on right-of-ways lined by mile after mile of waxy-green orange groves, went through Covina, Claremont, Upland, Etiwanda, and Rialto en route to San Bernardino, Redlands, and Riverside — more than sixty miles from Los Angeles.

From San Bernardino, the Pacific Electric climbed into its second mountain range with tracks to the San Bernardino Mountain resort of Arrowhead Springs. (Its first range was the San Gabriels, reached with the Mount Lowe line.)

The P. E.'s four-track line stretching southward from Los Angeles was a busy route. The line went directly to Long Beach, which by now had grown into a city and was developing a port. From this line, one branch went to Whittier, Yorba Linda, and Fullerton; one went to Santa Ana; another cut down the coast to Huntington Beach and Newport Beach, and others went to San Pedro, Redondo Beach, Gardena, and El Segundo.

ABOVE: A Pacific Electric train stops on Garey Avenue near Third in Pomona after service there began in 1912. (Pomona Public Library) BELOW: A Big Red Car waits in Covina in 1907. (Craig Rasmussen Collection)

ABOVE: Poles with trolley wires went down the middle of Ocean Boulevard in Long Beach in the mid-1920's. This scene is near Pine Avenue. (Title Insurance and Trust Co.) BELOW: Cars for Long Beach and Pasadena are leaving the P. E. 6th and Main station, Los Angeles, in this 1910 photograph. (Craig Rasmussen Collection)

Other routes went from Los Angeles to Santa Monica, Beverly Hills, Venice, Playa del Rey, Glendale, Burbank, Hollywood, Pasadena, South Pasadena, Sierra Madre, San Marino, Arcadia, Monrovia and Covina.

Interurbans left as frequently as every seven minutes during rush hours. Some trains were composed of as many as four Big Red Cars coupled together.

The P. E. also operated "local" streetcar service in many cities, including San Pedro, Long Beach, Pasadena, Los Angeles, Pomona, Riverside, San Bernardino, Redlands, and Santa Ana. They ranged from Birney "one man" cars on which the motorman also collected fares to large trolleys with center entrances that became familiar on Hollywood Boulevard.

Passengers purchased interurban tickets, including bargain commuter "passes," at P. E. stations in the larger cities. Those who boarded trains elsewhere could buy tickets from conductors, who indicated each rider's destination by placing punched "checks" in slots on seats or by windows. Patrons on "local" service trolleys usually dropped coins in the fare box.

Rush hours frequently found standing room only on the cars. The interurbans used on the

Used until the mid-1920's, the Pacific Electric's Hill Street station was between 4th and 5th. Adjoining is the Masonic Temple, once used for the Los Angeles Pacific offices. (Security Pacific National Bank)

longer lines carried sixty to eighty passengers, while trolleys used on short "local" routes provided seats for as few as twenty-eight passengers. Almost from the start of P. E. service, the interurbans were called "Big Red Cars."

During this era, the Pacific Electric's slogan, "Ride the Big Red Cars," was popularized with billboards, newspaper advertising, imprinting on timetables, and placards on and in the trolleys themselves.

The nerve center of P. E. operations was the Pacific Electric Building at Sixth and Main Streets in downtown Los Angeles. The structure housed not only the firm's general offices, but also was the place of arrival and departure for most of the Big Red Cars. Some interurbans rolled out of the building directly onto Main Street, while others used elevated tracks to go from the station to San Pedro Street.

Despite more modern and faster interurbans, trips were requiring more time during the 1920's. Roads for the increasing numbers of automobiles were being cut through Pacific Electric right-of-ways, forcing the interurbans to reduce speed to avoid collisions. Trolleys using tracks that unfortunately had been laid on public streets also moved slower because of the additional autos.

When the trolley operators began losing time on the streets, they tried to go over — and under — the barriers. In 1909, the Los Angeles and Pacific Railroad began using tunnels it cut through Bunker Hill. The Pacific Electric started using elevated tracks to carry interurbans from San Pedro Street to its Sixth and Main station in 1910.

But the P. E.'s most ambitious project to reduce travel time though downtown Los Angeles streets was the Hollywood Subway. It began beneath the Subway Terminal Building on Hill Street between Fourth and Fifth Streets and carried trolleys four-fifths of a mile to a point near First Street and Glendale Boulevard. From there, interurbans travelled to Hollywood, Glendale, Burbank, the San Fernando Valley, and Santa Monica Bay communities. The tunnel was used until 1955.

During the mid-1920's, the Pacific Electric could boast that 2,400 trains were scheduled daily. In 1924, Big Red Cars carried 109,185,650 passengers, its all-time rail record. The gross P. E. revenue that year was $20,729,483.

Despite these receipts, the Pacific Electric lost $592,185 in 1924 and through most of its existence operated at a deficit. In attempts to show a profit, schedules were increased and decreased, and fares were boosted and offered at bargain rates. Most efforts to show a profit were in vain, although the P. E. did make money during World War II when freight and passenger service increased sharply.

Henry Huntington founded a trolley empire and also developed electric power companies.

Even though the Pacific Electric hit a peak during the 1920's, its rail service began to wane during the last part of the decade. In 1927, the P. E. started using buses and cutting back on rail service.

In that same year that bus service began, ironically, Henry E. Huntington died. The years following the sale of his electric railroad properties had been active ones for him.

Huntington's sale of the interurban empire did not mean that he was retiring. He was the principal stockholder in the Los Angeles Light and Power Company, which eventually merged with the Southern California Edison Company. (For details, see *The Railroad That Lighted Southern California*, by Hank Johnston; Los Angeles: 1967.) Huntington also owned the profitable Los Angeles Railway Company, the narrow gauge (3'6") local service streetcar system. In addition, he held valuable land parcels acquired at bargain prices while building the electric railroads.

Henry Huntington's greatest pleasure evidently came from assembling rare book and art treasures for the Huntington Library and Art Gallery, established at his palatial San Marino estate. Outbidding other collectors, Hunt-

P. E. dominated Brand Boulevard, Glendale's main street, in 1924. (Security Pacific National Bank)

THE SILK STORE
REAL ESTATE
REALTOR
4 Floors of Music
Music

Huntington donated his family home in Oneonta, N. Y. for a public library. (Photo by the Author)

ington purchased such art works as Gainsborough's "Blue Boy" and Lawrence's "Pinkie." He also acquired an original folio of Shakespeare's plays, the manuscript of Benjamin Franklin's autobiography, a Gutenberg Bible, and thousands of rare books.

The library and art gallery, a non-profit foundation, was made available for scholarly research. The facility was also opened for public tours.

The Pacific Electric began nearing the end of the line during the 1930's. More people owned automobiles, and new highways pushed through the electric railroad's right-of-way. Invasion of the tracks forced the Big Red Cars to continually reduce speeds to avoid accidents. Slower schedules caused passengers to turn to autos or buses.

The Depression of the 1930's brought vast unemployment, and many commuters no longer had jobs. In 1933, the P. E. carried only 67,695,352 passengers, a drop of 42 million from 1924. The company had been losing money almost since it was organized, and the Depression brought even deeper deficits.

The Pacific Electric also was badly in need of new trolleys, a California State Railroad Commission report said in 1939. Some interurbans in use at the time had been purchased in 1902 by Huntington! The prices of trolleys soared during the years. The cars for the initial interurban line to Pasadena cost $3,500; the last new trolleys acquired by the Pacific Electric were Presidents Conference Car "streamliners" costing more than $30,000 each in 1940.

Pointing to the high costs of modernizing tracks and buying new trolleys, the P. E. in 1939 won state approval to substitute bus service on several rail routes. Only the start of World War II, with tire and gasoline shortages, kept the firm from abandoning more rail routes. During the war, patronage climbed sharply; in 1945, the P. E. carried 177,996,137 passengers (109,124,721 of them by rail). However, when the war ended, the remaining Big Red Cars were more antiquated than ever and the discontinuance of rail service resumed.

Meanwhile the state started a massive program of freeway construction. Most of the first freeways paralleled the routes of the Big Red Cars, indicating how definitely the electric railroad lines influenced Southern California's growth. When the Cahuenga Pass freeway was constructed in the late 1940's, it was divided by a two-track trolley line serving the San Fernando Valley. This arrangement might well have served as a pattern for developing all freeways to include rail transit lines. The cost of acquiring the small amount of additional land for such service would have been small as compared to building rapid transit lines alone.

Unfortunately, the tracks were removed from Cahuenga Pass and allowances never were made for such lines in the other freeways.

The Pacific Electric sold its passenger service effective October 1, 1953, to Metropolitan Coach Lines, a firm specializing in operating buses. This company obtained state authorization to discontinue electric car service to Glendale and Hollywood in 1955, but continued to operate trolleys to Long Beach, Bellflower, and

San Pedro. Succeeding this private firm in operating buses and the remaining interurbans was the Metropolitan Transit Authority, a public agency that took over the chore of carrying passengers on March 3, 1958. It discontinued rail service to Bellflower in 1958 and to San Pedro in 1959.

The only interurban service remaining was between Los Angeles and Long Beach, which coincidentally was the first line built by Huntington.

Despite technological advances, the line to Long Beach was not operating as efficiently as it did under Henry Huntington. If highway planners had crossed over or under the tracks instead of through them, efficient service might have continued. In 1910, for example, the Big Red Cars left every twenty minutes and made the trip in forty-one minutes! By the late 1950's, cars ran every half hour and were scheduled to reach their destination in an hour—but usually were ten to thirty minutes late.

Frosted windows in this San Bernardino-bound car show the location of lavatories, used only on long-run P. E. lines. (Photograph by Vernon J. Sappers) BELOW: a car rolls to San Pedro soon after opening of two extra tracks in 1907. (Pacific Railway Journal)

P. E. cars once rolled on Hollywood Boulevard, shown in the 1940's as a trolley passed Grauman's Chinese Theater. (Southern California Visitors Bureau)

Even though service had eroded, commuters still liked the Big Red Cars. The transit authority's announcement that it planned to discontinue service brought petitions and threats of law suits — all to no avail.

Big Red Car service ended April 8, 1961.

The last interurban arrived in Long Beach shortly after midnight, and appropriately carried a contingent of Big Red Car fans.

The streetcar service of the Los Angeles Railway Company fared slightly better. The company was owned by the Huntington estate until 1944, when it was sold to National City Lines. The new owners renamed the system Los Angeles Transit Lines and began substituting buses for trolleys. The lines were acquired by the Metropolitan Transit Authority when it was formed in 1958. The authority discontinued the remaining streetcar service on March 31, 1963, and began running buses on the routes.

A particularly tragic aspect of the end of Los Angeles streetcar service was the fact that trolley lines served low income areas where Negroes and Mexican-Americans resided. The end of trolley service providing relatively efficient and low-priced travel made it extremely difficult for these people to commute to jobs.

The Metropolitan Transit Authority was replaced in 1964 by a new public organization, the Southern California Rapid Transit District — a unit that operated only buses and appeared to be "rapid" only in its name. Its buses, seemingly immune from the police as they frequently violated speed and highway safety laws, helped increase traffic jams on already crowded streets and freeways.

The City of Southern California, shaped economically and sociologically so greatly by the Pacific Electric's Big Red Cars, found itself facing perplexing inconsistencies in the late twentieth century.

Millions of dollars in public funds were being used to convert the antiquated liner Queen Mary into a garish tourist "attraction," yet little was being done to modernize its decaying downtown district or, more important, eliminate its ghettos and poor housing.

Washing the dirt off trolleys to keep the Big Red Cars sparkling was one of the chores at the end of a day's run. The operation here is taking place in Long Beach. (Photo by Maxine Reams)

Southern California's first freeways paralleled P. E. lines, which set city patterns. ABOVE: This train heads south by the Long Beach Freeway. (Photo by the Author) BELOW: Fans ride a car to the port where it was junked when service was ending in 1959.

Mile after mile of new homes were being built on the farmlands once traversed by the Big Red Cars, yet there were practically no standards to require developers to relinquish part of their huge profits and provide parks that would help avoid creating a new kind of slums.

Despite the manifold problems accompanying the population and industrial growth, public funds that should be spent to solve the tragedies of crowded schools, packed recreational facilities, busy highways, and increased tax loads on homeowners still were being given to the Southern California Visitors Council and many Chambers of Commerce to attract even more residents and undesirable industries.

Though part of the smog problem was blamed on the great number of automobiles — most of them carrying only a single rider — used by commuters, no concerted moves were being made to develop rapid transit under the patterns of New York City, Boston, Philadelphia, Cleveland, Chicago, San Francisco, Montreal, Toronto or Mexico City.

Even though adequate public transportation was a prime need for most Southern Californians, the politicians and business leaders controlling the area's destiny helped direct millions of dollars into "cultural" development almost inaccessible to the average person because of travel difficulties, yet failed to push construction of a rapid transit system.

And what happened to the trolleys and rights-of-ways?

The Orange Empire Trolley Museum in Perris preserved many interurbans and streetcars so that the children who never had the pleasure of riding electric railroads could enjoy short trips. Some interurbans were crushed for scrap metal, while others went overseas to nations still using trolley cars.

Many of the rights-of-ways were consolidated into part of the Southern Pacific to haul freight. A few, such as the one dividing Sierra Madre Avenue in San Marino, Pasadena, and Sierra Madre, were planted with grass and flowers for beautification. Houses unjudiciously were crowded onto the vacated right-of-way adjoining Appian Way in Long Beach. After removal of the tracks between Seal Beach and Huntington Beach, the right-of-way became a seaside state park. Highway building programs engulfed some right-of-ways.

The question probably always will arise as to why the Pacific Electric system wasn't preserved to operate as a publicly-owned agency.

One reason undoubtedly was a general fear

The Pacific Electric's Long Beach line at Dominguez was typical of the system's well-built right-of-way. (Charles Lawrence Photo: Charles Seims Collection)

that taxes would be required to subsidize its operation. Even if this were true, such funds would be considerably less than the vast — and seemingly endless — expenditures on freeways which became crowded and outdated almost as soon as completed.

The P. E. network as it existed would never serve modern needs, but it would have been an excellent and bargain-priced starting place for a rapid transit system. Among its faults was its use of public streets, but it would have been more economical to re-route such sections via subways or private right-of-ways than to have abandoned all trackage.

The Pacific Electric's sharp curves could have been straightened to serve high-speed electric cars, and under or over passes could easily have been built to carry tracks away from highway crossings.

Southern Californians bemoan automobile traffic and cry for a rapid transit system.

Historians of the future may ponder the question of why they didn't keep the one they had.

◻

These Pacific Electric cars, piled high for junking at Terminal Island in Los Angeles Harbor in 1959, looked like toys. Riders turned to buses; streets became more crowded. (Photo by Maxine Reams)

A PHOTO ALBUM

EDWARDS
WILDEY
HOTEL
LAMM

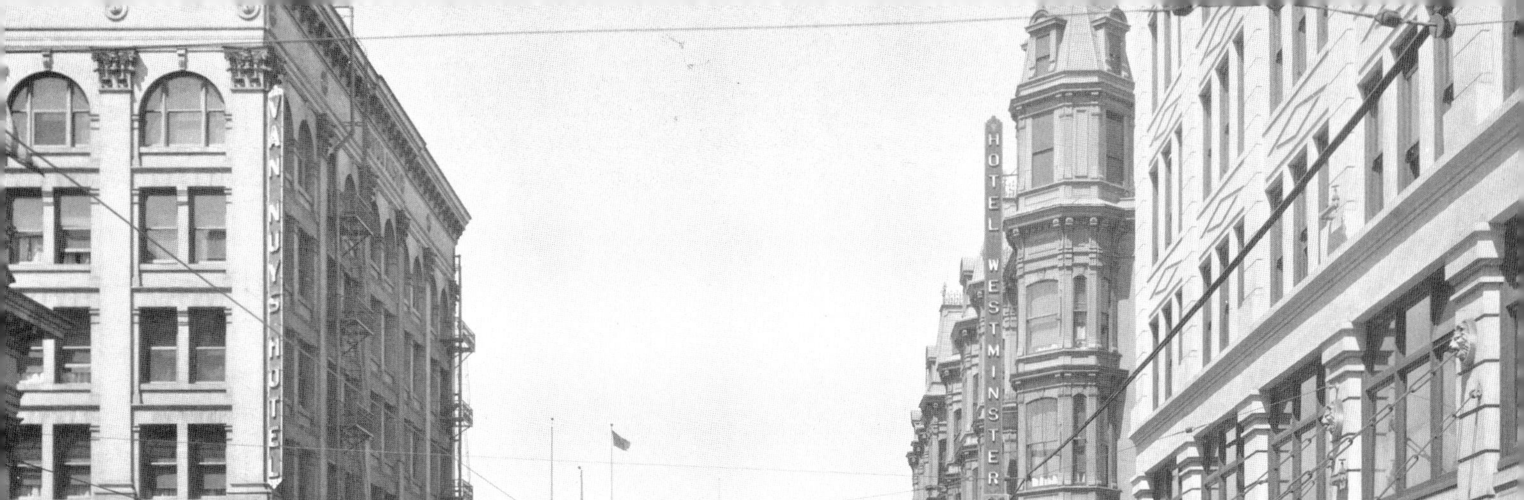

Virtually every downtown Los Angeles street had streetcar tracks during the 1920's, peak of the trolley era. Commuters used the Pacific Electric's Big Red Cars to travel in relative comfort from suburban homes to jobs in Los Angeles. ABOVE: A Sierra Madre-bound interurban heads north on Main Street in 1924. (Title Insurance and Trust Company Collection) RIGHT: This 1930 picture made at 6th and Hill Street shows a P. E. Car with center doors designed to expedite passengers' entry and exit. (Security Pacific National Bank Collection.)

Operating on downtown Los Angeles streets slowed cars on many P. E. lines. ABOVE: An electric car on Broadway approaches 2nd Street. (Craig Rasmussen Collection) BELOW: A narrow-gauge Los Angeles Railway car waits for traffic on Broadway and 7th in 1930. (Security Pacific National Bank)

Hollywood was served by the Los Angeles Pacific Railroad, which in 1911 was merged into the Pacific Electric. Farmlands turned into a city around trolleys. ABOVE: An electric car rolls west on Hollywood Boulevard at Highland in 1905. The Hollywood Hotel is left center. (Los Angeles County Museum of Natural History) RIGHT: A trolley operates through Cahuenga Pass, connecting Hollywood with the San Fernando Valley. (Stephen D. Maguire Collection) Below: Cars on Santa Monica Boulevard are approaching Western Avenue in this 1922 scene. (Security Pacific National Bank Historical Collection)

A variety of trolley lines served Hollywood. ABOVE: A Birney car, designed for one-man operation, moves past William Fox Studios on Western Avenue near Sunset Boulevard in 1922. BELOW: A Santa Monica-Venice car goes west on Hollywood Boulevard in 1929. (Both Photos: Security Pacific National Bank)

ABOVE: *This Hollywood Boulevard "local" service car enters the subway to downtown Los Angeles in this picture made during the 1940's. (Pacific Railroad Publications)* BELOW: *A 1930 view shows a trolley moving east on Santa Monica Boulevard; another car waits on Western. (Security Pacific National Bank)*

LINES OF THE PACIFIC ELECT

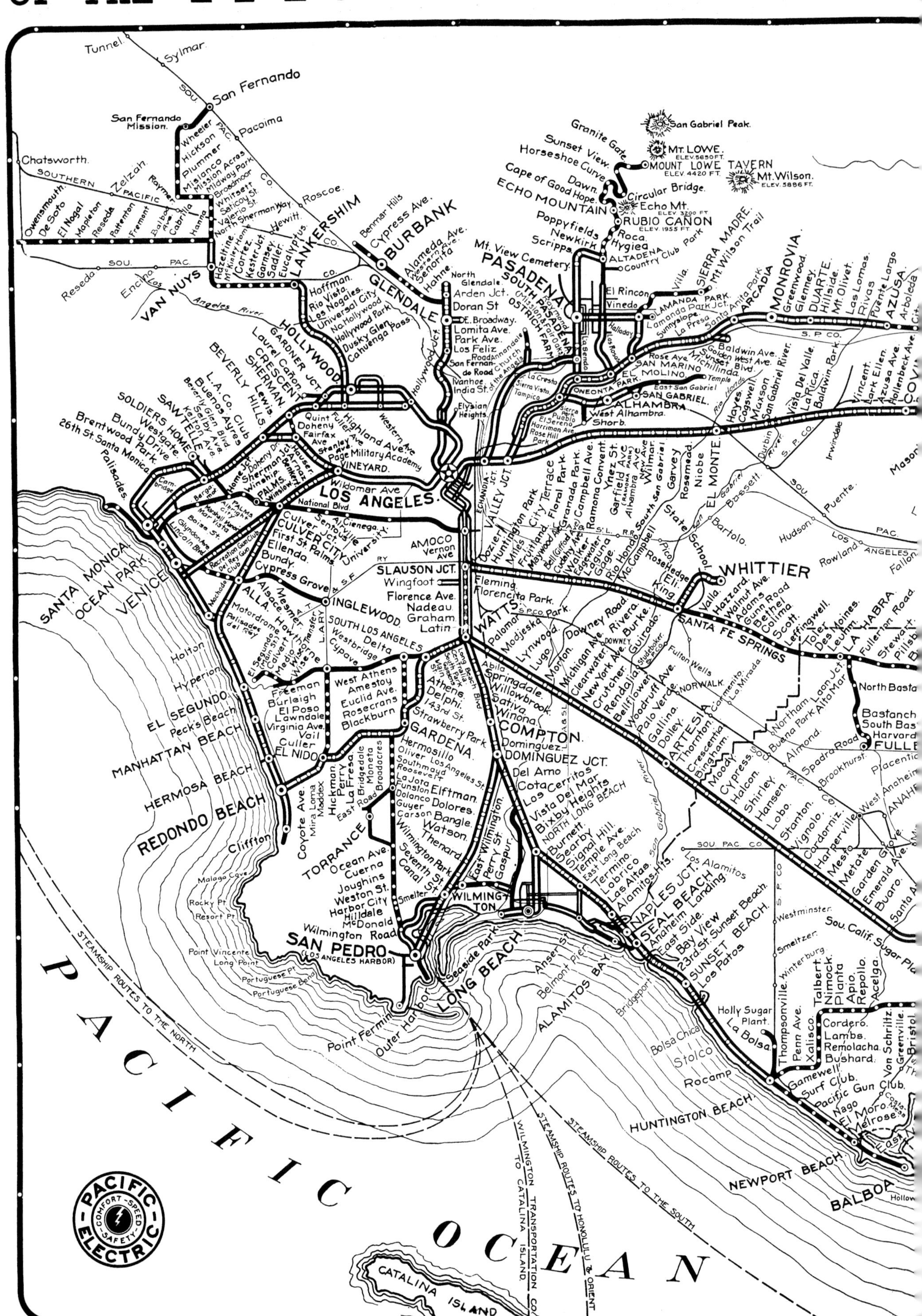

C RAILWAY IN SOUTHERN CALIFORNIA

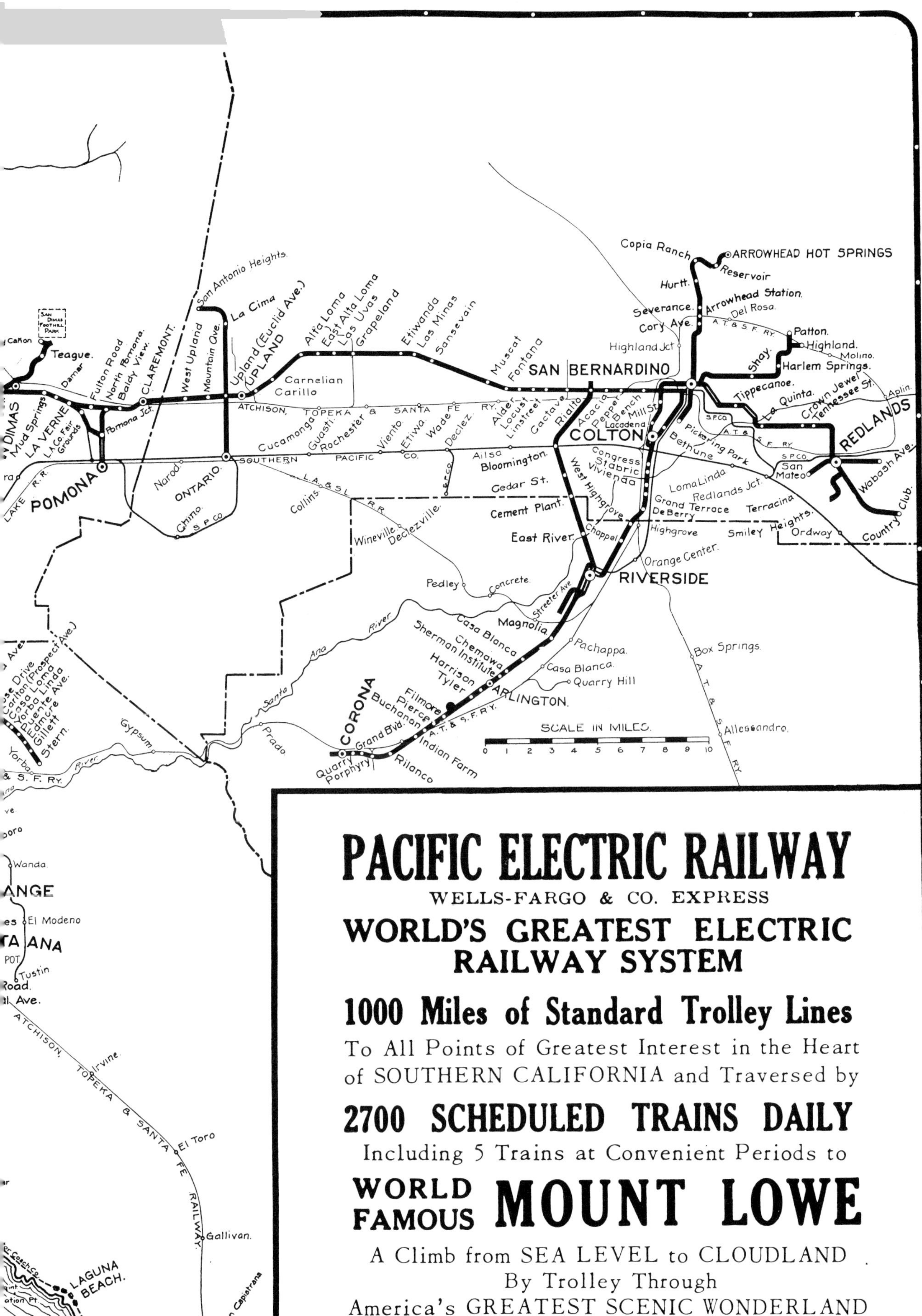

PACIFIC ELECTRIC RAILWAY

WELLS-FARGO & CO. EXPRESS

WORLD'S GREATEST ELECTRIC RAILWAY SYSTEM

1000 Miles of Standard Trolley Lines

To All Points of Greatest Interest in the Heart of SOUTHERN CALIFORNIA and Traversed by

2700 SCHEDULED TRAINS DAILY

Including 5 Trains at Convenient Periods to

WORLD FAMOUS MOUNT LOWE

A Climb from SEA LEVEL to CLOUDLAND
By Trolley Through
America's GREATEST SCENIC WONDERLAND

SAN BERNARDINO—RIVERSIDE—POMONA—SAN DIMAS—COVINA LINE

WESTBOUND TRAINS

STATIONS	Miles	†	*	*	L*§	†	*	L*	*	L*	*	‡	*	*	*	*	*	L*f	*	*	L*	*	*	L*	*	*	*	L*
Highland (cS.B.)	.00							6 00		7 10					10 15			1 10			3 10			4 15				7 15
Arrowhead Hot Spgs. (cS.B.)	.00									7 04								1 04			3 34			3 34				5 34
Redlands (cS.B.)	.00							6 05		7 10					10 05			1 10			3 15			4 15				7 10
Colton (cS.B.)	.00							6 23		7 29					10 11			1 15			3 11			4 06				7 11
San Bernardino	.00							6 40		7 40		8 40			10 50			1 45			4 05			5 15				7 50
Riverside	.00							6 25		7 25					10 30			1 25			3 50			5 00				t7 30
Bloomington	6.66							6 42		7 42					10 47			1 42			4 07			5 17				t7 48
Rialto	4.47							6 51		7 51		8 50			11 01			1 55			4 16			5 26				8 01
Fontana	8.22							7 02		8 02		8 57			11 10			2 05			4 27			5 35				8 10
Etiwanda	12.68							7 10		8 10		9 05			11 18			2 13			4 35			5 43				8 18
Alta Loma	18.00							7 17		8 17		9 12			11 25			2 20			4 42			5 50				8 25
Upland (Euclid Ave.)	21.48							7 24		8 25		9 19			11 32			2 27			4 50			5 57				8 32
Ontario (cU) Ar. from East)	.00							7 37		8 37		9 37			11 42			2 39			5 04			6 09				9 13
Ontario (cU) (Lv. for West)								7 12		8 12					11 12			2 12			4 38			5 42				8 12
Claremont	25.47							7 33		8 33					11 40			2 34			4 58			6 05				8 40
North Pomona	27.06							7 37		8 37					11 44			2 38			5 01			6 09				8 44
Pomona (Ar. from East)	.00							7 50		8 50					11 58			2 52			5 21			6 21				9 04
Pomona (Lv. for West)					6 25			7 28		8 22	8 35		9 54		11 30	12 40		2 23	2 50	3 50	4 47			5 37		6 38		8 26
Pomona Jct.	.00				6 31						8 41		10 00			12 46			2 56	3 56						6 44		
Lordsburg	28.63				6 37			7 41		8 41	8 47		10 06		11 48	12 52		2 42	3 02	4 02	5 04			6 13		6 50		8 48
San Dimas (P. E.)	.00				6 37			7 42		8 42			10 08		11 41	12 53		2 40		4 04	5 06			5 54			7 52	
San Dimas (S. P.)	31.48				6 42			7 46		8 46	8 53		10 12		11 53	12 57		2 47	3 07	4 07	5 09			6 19		6 55		8 54
Covina (Citrus Ave.)	35.69		5 46	6 39	6 53		7 26	7 57	8 11	8 57	9 04		10 23	11 01	12 04	1 08		2 58	3 18	4 18	5 20	5 25	5 56	6 30		7 06	8 04	9 05
Baldwin Park	40.23		5 57	6 50	7 04		7 38		8 22		9 15		10 34	11 12	12 13	1 19			3 29	4 29		5 37	6 07			7 17	8 15	
El Monte	44.70	5 50	6 07	7 00		7 15	7 47		8 32		9 25		10 44	11 22	12 23	1 29	2 41		3 39	4 39		5 47	6 17		6 55	7 27	8 25	
Wilmar	47.90	5 56	6 13	7 06		7 21	7 53		8 38		9 31		10 50	11 28	12 29	1 35	2 47		3 45	4 45		5 53	6 23		7 01	7 33	8 31	
Ramona Park	49.26	6 00	6 17	7 10		7 25	7 57		8 42		9 35		10 54	11 32	12 33	1 39	2 51		3 49	4 49		5 57	6 27		7 05	7 37	8 35	
Granada Park	51.01	6 04	6 21	7 14		7 29	8 01		8 46		9 39		10 58	11 36	12 37	1 43	2 55		3 53	4 53		6 01	6 31		7 09	7 41	8 39	
Covina Jct.	54.30	6 13	6 28	7 23	7 28	7 40	8 10	8 30	8 55	9 30	9 48		11 07	11 45	12 46	1 52	3 04	3 31	4 02	5 02	5 52	6 10	6 40	7 03	7 18	7 50	8 48	9 38
Los Angeles (Main St. Sta.)	57.41	6 28	6 43	7 38	7 43	7 55	8 25	8 45	9 11	9 45	10 04		11 23	12 01	1 02	2 08	3 20	3 47	4 18	5 18	6 03	6 26	6 56	7 20	7 35	8 06	9 05	9 55

STATIONS	*	*	*						
Highland (cS.B.)			9 40						
Arrowhead Hot Spgs. (cS.B.)			7 34						
Redlands (cS.B.)			9 15						
Colton (cS.B.)			9 39						
San Bernardino			10 46						
Riverside			t10 25						
Bloomington			t10 44						
Rialto			10 56						
Fontana			11 03						
Etiwanda			11 11						
Alta Loma			11 18						
Upland (Euclid Ave.)			11 25						
Ontario (cU) Ar. from East)			11 37						
Ontario (cU) (Lv. for West)			11 12						
Claremont			11 32						
North Pomona			11 35						
Pomona (Ar. from East)			11 47						
Pomona (Lv. for West)		9 40	11 20						
Pomona Jct.		9 46							
Lordsburg		9 52	11 39						
San Dimas (P. E.)	9 20								
San Dimas (S. P.)		9 58	11 44						
Covina (Citrus Ave.)	9 32	10 09	11 55						
Baldwin Park	9 43	10 20	12 05						
El Monte	9 53	10 30	12 14						
Wilmar	9 59	10 36	12 20						
Ramona Park	10 03	10 40	12 24						
Granada Park	10 07	10 44	12 28						
Covina Jct.	10 16	10 53	12 37						
Los Angeles (Main St. Sta.)	10 33	11 10	12 54						

* Daily. † Daily except Sunday. cS B Connection at San Bernardino. cU Connections at Upland (Euclid Ave.). Time shown at Ontario is arrival by nearest connecting train. t Transfer to or from Riverside and Bloomington at Rialto. ‡ Daily except Saturday, Sunday or Holidays. § Makes all stops east of Hayes, leaving Hayes 7:12 A. M. runs limited Hayes to Los Angeles. L Limited Train makes no stops between Los Angeles (Covina Junction) and Covina. f Stop on signal at Ynez and Ramona Park. Light figures A. M. Dark figures P. M.

LOS ANGELES—COVINA—SAN DIMAS

NORTH

STATIONS	Miles	*	*	*	*	*	*	*	*	*	*	*	*	*	*	*	*	‡	*	*	*	*	
Los Angeles	0	5 10	6 20	7 10	8 00	8 50	9 30	10 30	11 30	12 30	1 00	2 00	2 50	3 30	4 10	4 50	5 20	5 50	6 20	8 00	9 30	11 45	
Covina Jct.	3.13	5 27	6 37	7 27	8 17	9 07	9 47	10 47	11 47	12 47	1 17	2 17	3 07	3 47	4 27	5 07	5 37	6 07	6 37	8 17	9 47	12 02	
City Limits	3.87	5 29	6 39	7 29	8 19	9 09	9 49	10 49	11 49	12 49	1 19	2 19	3 09	3 49	4 29	5 09	5 39	6 09	6 39	8 19	9 49	12 04	
Granada Park	6.40	5 33	6 43	7 33	8 23	9 13	9 53	10 53	11 53	12 53	1 23	2 23	3 13	3 53	4 33	5 13	5 43	6 13	6 43	8 23	9 53	12 08	
Ramona Conv.	7.29	5 35	6 45	7 35	8 25	9 15	9 55	10 55	11 55	12 55	1 25	2 25	3 15	3 55	4 35	5 15	5 45	6 15	6 45	8 25	9 55	12 10	
Wilmar	9.51	5 41	6 51	7 41	8 31	9 21	10 01	11 01	12 01	1 01	1 31	2 31	3 21	4 01	4 41	5 21	5 51	6 21	6 51	8 31	10 01	12 16	
El Monte	13.14	5 49	6 59	7 49	8 39	9 29	10 09	11 09	12 09	1 09	1 39	2 39	3 29	4 09	4 49	5 29	5 59	6 29	6 59	8 39	10 09	12 24	
Baldwin Park	17.58	5 59	7 09	7 59	8 49	9 39	10 19	11 19	12 19	1 19	1 49	2 49	3 39	4 19	4 59	5 39	6 09		7 09	8 49	10 19	12 34	
Covina	21.78	6 10	7 20	8 10	9 00	9 50	10 30	11 30	12 30	1 30	2 00	3 00	3 50	4 30	5 10	5 50	6 20		7 20	9 00	10 30	12 45	
San Dimas	26.86	6 22			9 12			11 42			2 12			4 42			6 32					12 57	

SAN DIMAS—COVINA—LOS ANGELES

SOUTH

STATIONS	Miles	*	*	*	*	*	*	*	*	*	*	*	*	*	*	*	*	*e	*	*	*	*	
San Dimas	0		6 26			9 16			11 46			2 16			4 46				6 36				
Covina	5.08	5 48	6 38	7 38	8 28	9 28	10 30	11 30	11 58	12 58	1 48	2 28	3 08	3 50	4 58	5 18	5 58		6 48	7 58	9 08	10 38	
Baldwin Park	9.28	5 58	6 48	7 48	8 38	9 38	10 40	11 40	12 08	1 08	1 58	2 38	3 18	4 00	5 08	5 28	6 08		6 58	8 08	9 18	10 48	
El Monte	13.72	6 09	6 59	7 59	8 49	9 49	10 51	11 51	12 19	1 19	2 09	2 49	3 29	4 11	5 19	5 39	6 19	6 50	7 09	8 19	9 29	10 59	
Wilmar	17.35	6 16	7 06	8 06	8 56	9 56	10 58	11 58	12 26	1 26	2 16	2 56	3 36	4 18	5 26	5 46	6 26	6 57	7 16	8 26	9 36	11 06	
Ramona Conv.	19.57	6 22	7 12	8 12	9 02	10 02	11 04	12 04	12 32	1 32	2 22	3 02	3 42	4 24	5 32	5 52	6 32	7 03	7 22	8 32	9 42	11 12	
Granada Park	20.46	6 24	7 14	8 14	9 04	10 04	11 06	12 06	12 34	1 34	2 24	3 07	3 44	4 26	5 34	5 54	6 34	7 05	7 24	8 34	9 44	11 14	
City Limits	22.99	6 27	7 17	8 17	9 07	10 07	11 09	12 09	12 37	1 37	2 27	3 04	3 47	4 29	5 37	5 57	6 37	7 08	7 27	8 37	9 47	11 17	
Covina Jct.	23.73	6 29	7 19	8 19	9 09	10 09	11 11	12 11	12 39	1 39	2 29	3 09	3 49	4 31	5 39	5 59	6 39	7 10	7 29	8 39	9 49	11 19	
Los Angeles	26.86	6 48	7 38	8 38	9 28	10 28	11 28	12 28	12 58	1 58	2 48	3 28	4 08	4 48	5 58	6 18	6 58	7 27	7 48	8 58	10 08	11 38	

* Daily. † Wilmar only; daily except Sunday. ‡ To El Monte only. ¶ Wilmar to Los Angeles only. e El Monte to Los Angeles. Light figures A. M. Dark figures P. M Extra service Sundays and Holidays according to requirements of travel. Cars on this line do no work south of Covina Junction.

The Big Red Car also reigned in the Orange Empire. ABOVE: A 3-car train crosses the Santa Ana River en route to Corona. (Photograph by Vernon J. Sappers) BELOW: A P. E. car going from Pomona to Los Angeles stops at Lordsburg (La Verne) while a Southern Pacific train passes. (Pomona Public Library)

Redlands, deep in the beautiful citrus country, received Pacific Electric interurban and "local" trolley service. Here a trolley stands on Orange Street, facing The Triangle in downtown Redlands, during the early 1900's. Streetcars went from downtown to the Smiley Heights residential district. (Redlands Daily Facts*)*

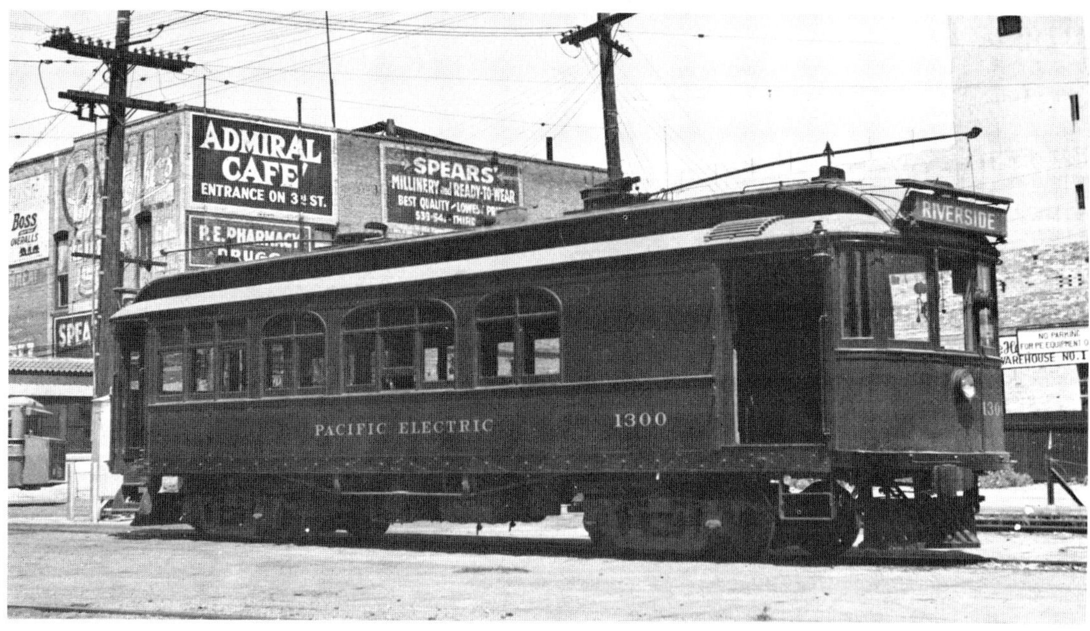

A car at the San Bernardino P. E. station prepares to leave for Riverside. (Photo by Vernon J. Sappers)

P. E. stations were built in a variety of styles. Some were little more than shelters, while others were elaborate. ABOVE LEFT: The La Verne station was faced with wood. (Pomona Public Library) ABOVE RIGHT: Lines popular during the 1910's distinguished the station at Upland. (Photograph by the Author) BELOW: The station at Claremont was regarded as one of the most beautiful in the sprawling 1,200-mile Pacific Electric system. It also served the Southern Pacific. (Pomona Public Library)

Some Big Red Cars were not so large! These open-air P. E. trolleys began providing "local" service in 1909, three years before fast interurbans connected the city to Los Angeles. (Pomona Public Library)

The high-speed line from Valley Junction east to San Bernardino operated with cars using 1200 volts, compared with 600 elsewhere on the system. ABOVE: A Covina car arrives at Valley Junction. BELOW: A train with cars adorned with yellow and orange bands added for a 1939 "modernization" program heads to San Bernardino. The cars, the P. E.'s fastest, could go 60 miles an hour. (Photos by Vernon J. Sappers)

San Bernardino, center of an inland P. E. network, was linked to Los Angeles in 1914. LEFT: A wooden car built during the early years of the twentieth century stops at the San Bernardino station. (Photo by Vernon J. Sappers) CENTER: A trolley in the city's "local" service is shown on Third near "D" Street en route to Base Line in 1905. (Security Pacific National Bank) BOTTOM: This car went between San Bernardino and Colton. (Photo by Vernon J. Sappers)

ABOVE: A Big Red Car with "porthole" windows waits at Arrowhead Springs beside a tank car carrying spring water. (Photo by Vernon J. Sappers) BELOW: A Pacific Electric car passes the Mission Inn at Main and 7th in Riverside. (Stephen D. Maguire Collection) The 10-ride "commutation ticket" (below) gave reduced prices over round trip fares.

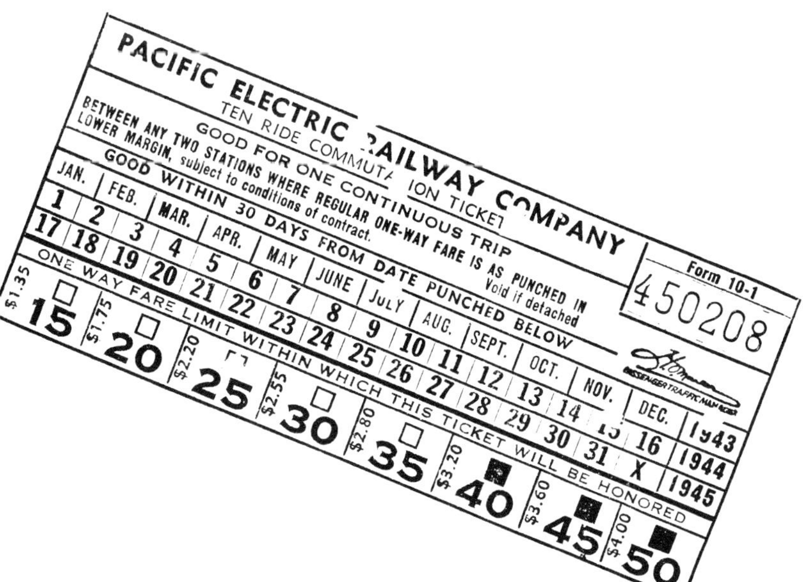
PACIFIC ELECTRIC RAILWAY COMPANY
TEN RIDE COMMUTATION TICKET
GOOD FOR ONE CONTINUOUS TRIP
BETWEEN ANY TWO STATIONS WHERE REGULAR ONE-WAY FARE IS AS PUNCHED IN LOWER MARGIN, subject to conditions of contract. Void if detached
GOOD WITHIN 30 DAYS FROM DATE PUNCHED BELOW
Form 10-1
450208
JAN. FEB. MAR. APR. MAY JUNE JULY AUG. SEPT. OCT. NOV. DEC.
1 2 3 4 5 6 7 8 9 10 11 12 13 14 15 16
17 18 19 20 21 22 23 24 25 26 27 28 29 30 31 X
1943 1944 1945
PASSENGER TRAFFIC MANAGER
ONE WAY FARE LIMIT WITHIN WHICH THIS TICKET WILL BE HONORED
$1.35 15 $1.75 20 $2.20 25 $2.55 30 $2.80 35 $3.20 40 $3.60 45 $4.00 50

MT. LOWE
WORLD FAMOUS

HIS Trolley Trip is unsurpassed by any mountain scenic ride in the world. Trains leave daily from Pacific Electric Station, Sixth and Main Sts., Los Angeles, at 8, 9 and 10 a. m. and 1:30 and 4 p. m. through Pasadena via Oak Knoll, Altadena and beautiful foot-hill hamlets, winding their way through orchards of oranges and beautiful country places and then up canyons by steep, curving ways to Rubio. Thence by an almost perpendicular ascent of the mountainside on the great incline railway, passengers are conveyed to Echo Mountain, attaining a height of 1325 feet in 3200 feet traveled. At Echo are the interesting Mt. Lowe Observatory and that "eye of night" the great searchlight. From Echo the journey continues 'round mountain walls, through forest and granite gates, mid scenes of ever changing grandeur to Alpine Tavern. This charming, mile-high mountain resort with its central hotel, dining room and cottages among the pines, is a delightful haven of rest. Pony trains make trips to the summit 1100 feet above. Many points, within easy walk of Alpine, present wondrous views. Excursion Fare of $2.00 now available for a limited time. ($1.75 from Pasadena.) Excursion Fare Tickets must be purchased from Ticket Agents at Los Angeles or Pasadena. They will not be sold by Conductors on cars. Secure a folder.

The Mount Lowe trip, via interurban from Los Angeles to Altadena, cable car from Rubio Canyon to Echo Mountain, and then by narrow gauge trolley to the Alpine Lodge, was the P. E.'s most unusual line. ABOVE: Passengers enjoyed a magnificent view. A 1911 description and timetable provide details.

LOS ANGELES—ALTADENA—MT. LOWE N

STATIONS	Mls.	*	*	*	†	†	*	*
Los Angeles	0	8 00	9 00	10 00	....	....	1 30	4 00
Covina Junction	3.13	8 17	9 17	10 17	....	....	1 47	4 17
Sierra Vista	7.42	8 24	9 24	10 24	....	....	1 54	4 24
Oneonta Park	8.31	8 26	9 26	61 26	....	....	1 56	4 26
El Molino	10.04	8 30	9 30	10 30	....	....	2 00	4 30
Pasadena	13.00	8 50	9 50	10 50	12 00	1 00	2 20	4 50
Altadena	17.11	9 05	10 05	11 05	12 15	1 15	2 35	5 05
Rubio	18.88	9 15	10 15	11 15	12 25	1 25	2 45	5 15
Echo Mountain	19.38	9 25	10 25	11 25	12 35	1 35	2 55	5 25
Cape of Good Hope	20.25	9 30	10 30	11 30	12 40	1 40	3 00	5 30
Dawn	20.61	9 35	10 35	11 35	12 45	1 45	3 05	5 35
Circular Bridge	21.15	9 40	10 40	11 40	12 50	1 50	3 10	5 40
Granite Gate	22.00	9 46	10 46	11 46	12 56	1 56	3 16	5 46
Alpine Tavern	22.95	10 00	11 00	12 00	1 10	2 10	3 30	6 00

MT. LOWE—ALTADENA—LOS ANGELES S

STATIONS	Mls.	*	*	*	*	S		
Alpine Tavern	0	8 30	10 00	2 00	4 30	7 00	....	....
Granite Gate	95	8 36	10 06	2 06	4 36	7 06	....	....
Circular Bridge	1.80	8 46	10 16	2 16	4 46	7 16	....	....
Dawn	2.34	8 51	10 21	2 21	4 51	7 21	....	....
Cape of Good Hope	2.70	8 56	10 26	2 26	4 56	7 26	....	....
Echo Mountain	4.57	9 05	10 35	2 35	5 05	8 15	....	....
Rubio	5.07	9 15	10 45	2 55	5 15	8 25	....	....
Altadena	5.84	9 25	10 55	3 05	5 25	8 35	....	....
Pasadena	9.95	9 40	11 10	3 20	5 40	8 50	....	....
Raymond	11.45	....	....	3 26	5 47	....	....	....
Oneonta Park	12.84	....	....	3 33	5 52	....	....	....
Sierra Vista	13.73	....	....	3 35	5 54	....	....	....
Covina Junction	18.02	....	....	3 41	6 00	....	....	....
Los Angeles	21.15	10 25	11 55	3 52	6 17	9 35	....	....

Cars in this service northbound via Oak Knoll Line, southbound via Short Line.
* Daily. † Daily except Sunday. X Express M Mail. S Saturday, Sunday and Holidays. Light figures A.M. Dark figuret P.M. Extra service Sundays and Holidays according to requirements of travel.

A Reminiscence of Mt. Lowe

ABOVE: After the Mount Lowe Railway opened in 1893, its station was in the Pasadena Grand Opera House on South Raymond Avenue. Passengers rode carriages to Altadena, where they boarded narrow-gauge trolleys for Rubio Canyon. The P. E. acquired the mountain railroad in 1902 and launched through service to Los Angeles. (Charles Seims Collection) LEFT: Thaddeus Sobieski Coulincourt Lowe, the railway's builder, is pictured in the skull cap he wore in his later years. Lowe, born in 1832, was a man of many talents. In 1861, he built a balloon and flew 900 miles in it. President Lincoln named Lowe chief of the Army aeronautics corps, for which he developed observation balloons. Lowe invented a machine for making ice, regenerative metallic furnaces for gas and petroleum, and a coke oven system for producing gas and metallic coke. After investing a fortune in the Mount Lowe project, he was forced into bankruptcy. Heavily in debt, he died in 1913 at Pasadena.

ABOVE: A 1910 photo shows the start of the Mount Lowe incline railway at the Rubio Canyon pavilion, reached by interurbans. (Craig Rasmussen Collection) BELOW: A car nears the top of the incline. A fire in 1900 destroyed Echo Mountain House, in the background. The P. E. sketch shows the route from Los Angeles. Narrow-gauge trolleys carried passengers from Echo Mountain to the Mount Lowe Tavern.

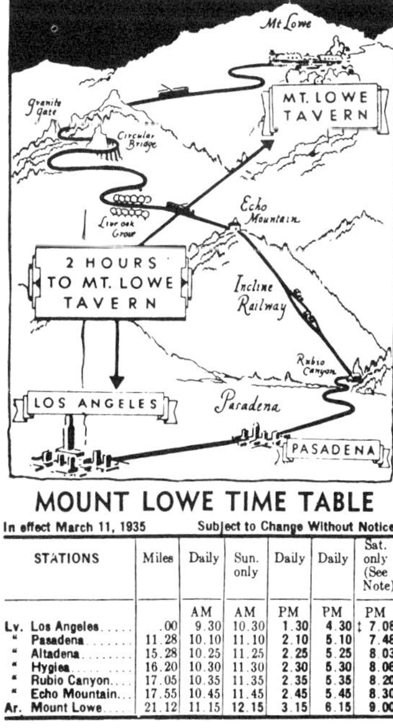

MOUNT LOWE TIME TABLE

In effect March 11, 1935 — Subject to Change Without Notice

	STATIONS	Miles	Daily	Sun. only	Daily	Daily	Sat. only (See Note)
			AM	AM	PM	PM	PM
Lv.	Los Angeles	.00	9.30	10.30	1.30	4.30	‡ 7.08
"	Pasadena	11.28	10.10	11.10	2.10	5.10	7.48
"	Altadena	15.28	10.25	11.25	2.25	5.25	8.03
"	Hygiea	16.20	10.30	11.30	2.30	5.30	8.08
"	Rubio Canyon	17.05	10.35	11.35	2.35	5.35	8.20
"	Echo Mountain	17.55	10.45	11.45	2.45	5.45	8.30
Ar.	Mount Lowe	21.12	11.15	12.15	3.15	6.15	9.00

LEFT: Passengers board a Mount Lowe incline railway cable car after arrival via interurban at the Rubio Canyon pavilion during the 1910's. (Pacific Railroad Publications) ABOVE: A pre-1900 sketch depicts a cable car arriving at the Echo Mountain House. BELOW: A P. E. folder used during the 1920's advertised the jaunt as the "greatest mountain trolley trip in the world." (Security Pacific National Bank Collection)

Here are two views of the modest station built after Echo Mountain House burned in 1900. ABOVE: The structure in the background of this earlier photograph is the observatory built by Lowe and destroyed by a windstorm in 1928. BELOW: This picture was made in the early 1930's, when the Mount Lowe trolleys still were carrying thousands of visitors annually. (Both Photos: Hank Johnston Collection)

A Mount Lowe trip highlight was the "Circular Bridge." Below: A car rounds the great curve in the 1920's. LEFT: An open-air trolley takes thrilled passengers around the bend on July 4, 1893, the day the Mount Lowe Railway opened. (Hank Johnston Collection) BELOW RIGHT: A more elaborate car operates in 1915 under P. E. ownership. (Craig Rasmussen Collection)

ABOVE: Trolleys rounded a 112 degree curve on "Circular Bridge," en route from Echo Mountain to Mount Lowe Tavern. There were 127 curves on the 3.27-mile line; travel time was a half hour. (Hank Johnston Collection) BELOW: A car stopped on one of the line's 18 bridges for this 1907 photo.

Altadena and Pasadena stretch into the smog-less distance in this view of the Mount Lowe Railway during the early twentieth century. Bigger trolleys eventually replaced this car. (Hank Johnston Collection)

Beautiful mountain scenery unfolded on the Mount Lowe Railway. ABOVE: A car nears Sentinel Rock in 1910. (Craig Rasmussen Collection) RIGHT: Trolleys were at three levels of the steep route when this photograph was made in the 1920's. (Pacific Electric) BELOW: This car, loaded with people, carried freight on the front. (Craig Rasmussen Collection)

The trolleys from Echo Mountain House carried passengers directly to the steps of Ye Alpine Tavern on Mount Lowe. Above: A car stands by the Tavern in approximately 1896, three years after it opened. (Craig Rasmussen Collection)

RIGHT: A car, with awning to shield passengers from the sun, is leaving the lodge. Fire destroyed the tavern in 1936. (Hank Johnston Collection)

Hairpin curves such as these were typical of the Mount Lowe railway. Service on the popular sightseeing line ended after a 1938 storm washed away major portions of the line. (Hank Johnston Collection)

An interurban with wooden sides waits by the cable railway in Rubio Canyon. BELOW: 1911 timetable showed more than 70 trains daily to Los Angeles. There were few paved roads in the area at the time.

PASADENA—LOS ANGELES—via SHORT LINE SOUTH

STATIONS	Miles	†	†	†	†	†	†	†	†F	†	†	†	†	†F	†	†	†	†F		
Pasadena—Colo. & Fair Oaks	0	5 10	6 00	6 20	6 40	7 00	7 12	7 22	7 32	7 42	7 54	8 03	8 20	8 35	8 48	9 00	9 15	9 30	9 45	10 00
Raymond	1.50	5 17	6 07	6 27	6 47	7 07	7 19	7 29	7 39	7 49	8 01	8 10	8 27	8 42	8 55	9 07	9 22	9 37	9 52	10 07
Mission and Fair Oaks	1.94	5 18	6 08	6 28	6 48	7 08	7 20	7 30	....	7 50	8 02	8 11	8 28	....	8 56	9 08	9 23	....	9 53	10 08
Oneonta Park	2.89	5 22	6 12	6 32	6 52	7 12	7 24	7 34	7 41	7 54	8 06	8 15	8 32	8 44	9 00	9 12	9 27	9 39	9 57	10 12
Sierra Vista	3.78	5 24	6 14	6 34	6 54	7 14	7 26	7 36	....	7 56	8 08	8 17	8 34	....	9 02	9 14	9 29	....	9 59	10 14
Covina Jct	8.07	5 31	6 21	6 41	7 01	7 21	7 33	7 43	....	8 03	8 15	8 24	8 41	....	9 09	9 21	9 36	....	10 06	10 21
Los Angeles	11.20	5 48	6 38	6 58	7 18	7 38	7 50	8 00	8 07	8 20	8 32	8 41	8 58	9 10	9 20	9 38	9 53	10 05	10 23	10 38

STATIONS	Miles	†	†	†	†	†	†	†	†	†	†	†	†	†	†	†	†	†
Pasadena—Colo. & Fair Oaks	0	10 15	10 30	10 45	11 00	11 15	11 30	11 45	12 00	12 20	12 40	1 00	1 15	1 30	1 45	2 00	2 15	2 30
Raymond	1.50	10 22	10 37	10 52	11 07	11 22	11 37	11 52	12 07	12 27	12 47	1 00	1 22	1 37	1 52	2 07	2 22	2 37
Mission and Fair Oaks	1.94	10 23	10 38	10 53	11 08	11 23	11 38	11 53	12 08	12 28	12 48	1 08	1 23	1 38	1 53	2 08	2 23	2 38
Oneonta Park	2.89	10 27	10 42	10 57	11 12	11 27	11 42	11 57	12 12	12 32	12 52	1 12	1 27	1 42	1 57	2 12	2 27	2 42
Sierra Vista	3.78	10 29	10 44	10 59	11 14	11 29	11 44	11 59	12 14	12 34	12 54	1 14	1 29	1 44	1 59	2 14	2 29	2 44
Covina Jct	8.07	10 36	10 51	11 06	11 21	11 36	11 51	12 06	12 21	12 41	1 01	1 21	1 36	1 51	2 06	2 21	2 36	2 51
Los Angeles	11.20	10 53	11 08	11 23	11 38	11 53	12 08	12 23	12 38	12 58	1 18	1 38	1 53	2 08	2 23	2 38	2 53	3 08

STATIONS	Miles	†	†	†	†	†	†	†	†	†	†	†	†	†	†	†	†	†	†	†
Pasadena—Colo. & Fair Oaks	0	2 45	2 56	3 06	3 16	3 26	3 36	3 46	3 54	4 02	4 10	4 17	4 25	4 32	4 37	4 48	4 58	5 08	5 18	5 28
Raymond	1.50	2 52	3 03	3 13	3 23	3 33	3 43	3 53	4 01	4 09	4 17	4 24	4 32	4 39	4 44	4 55	5 05	5 15	5 25	5 35
Mission and Fair Oaks	1.94	2 53	3 04	3 14	3 24	3 34	3 44	3 54	4 02	4 10	4 18	4 25	4 33	4 40	4 45	4 56	5 06	5 16	5 26	5 36
Oneonta Park	2.89	2 57	3 08	3 18	3 28	3 38	3 48	3 58	4 06	4 14	4 22	4 29	4 37	4 44	4 49	5 00	5 10	5 20	5 30	5 40
Sierra Vista	3.78	2 59	3 10	3 20	3 30	3 40	3 50	4 00	4 08	4 16	4 24	4 31	4 39	4 46	4 51	5 02	5 12	5 22	5 32	5 42
Covina Jct	8.07	3 06	3 17	3 24	3 37	3 47	3 57	4 07	4 15	4 23	4 31	4 38	4 46	4 53	4 58	5 09	5 19	5 29	5 39	5 49
Los Angeles	11.20	3 23	3 34	3 47	3 54	4 04	4 14	4 24	4 32	4 40	4 48	4 55	5 03	5 10	5 15	5 26	5 36	5 46	5 56	6 06

STATIONS	Miles	†	†	†	†	†	†	†	†	†	†	†	†	†	†	†	†	†	†
Pasadena—Colo. & Fair Oaks	0	5 38	5 48	6 00	6 10	6 20	6 30	6 45	7 05	7 20	7 40	8 15	8 45	9 15	9 45	10 15	10 45	11 15	11 45
Raymond	1.50	5 45	5 55	6 07	6 17	6 27	6 37	6 52	7 12	7 27	7 47	8 22	8 52	9 22	9 52	10 22	10 52	11 22	11 52
Mission and Fair Oaks	1.94	5 46	5 56	6 08	6 18	6 28	6 38	6 53	7 13	7 28	7 48	8 23	8 53	9 23	9 53	10 23	10 53	11 23	11 53
Oneonta Park	2.89	5 50	6 00	6 12	6 22	6 32	6 42	6 57	7 17	7 32	7 52	8 27	8 57	9 27	9 57	10 27	10 57	11 27	11 55
Sierra Vista	3.78	5 52	6 02	6 14	6 24	6 34	6 44	6 59	7 19	7 34	7 54	8 29	8 59	9 29	9 59	10 29	10 59	11 29	11 59
Covina Jct	8.07	5 59	6 09	6 21	6 31	6 41	6 51	7 06	7 26	7 41	8 01	8 36	9 06	9 36	10 06	10 36	11 06	11 36	12 06
Los Angeles	11.20	6 16	6 26	6 38	6 48	6 58	7 08	7 23	7 43	7 58	8 18	8 53	9 23	9 53	10 23	10 53	11 23	11 53	12 23

† Daily except Sunday. Light figures A. M. Dark figures P. M. Extra service Sundays and Holidays according to requirements of travel.

Pasadena, the prosperous San Gabriel Valley community which grew rapidly in the late nineteenth and early twentieth centuries, was blessed with a substantial network of trolley lines. The area's first electric interurban route linked the city to Los Angeles; lines stretched through Pasadena and surrounding areas. ABOVE: A Pasadena & Los Angeles Railway Co. trolley operates in 1896 on the first L.A.-Pasadena line, later part of the Pacific Electric. (Title Insurance and Trust Co.) LEFT: Fields surround this interurban, stopping in 1936 on the Pasadena Oak Knoll Line. (Stephen D. Maguire Collection) BELOW: A P. E. car, operating in 1906 on the Los Angeles-Pasadena line opened in 1895, nears the Los Angeles & Salt Lake Railroad tracks. (Security Pacific National Bank)

ABOVE: This photo of Colorado Street, Pasadena's main business artery, shows how trolleys dominated the business artery in the 1920's. BELOW: A trolley on Fair Oaks at Colorado in Pasadena takes passengers to Cawston Ostrich Farm, an attraction of the early 1900's. (Security Pacific National Bank)

ABOVE: P. E. cars with wooden bodies were built early in the twentieth century and were still in use in 1947. The scene is Colorado Street in Pasadena. (Photograph by Vernon J. Sappers) BELOW: A 3-car train returns to the yards after a day's service. Note the extensive right-of-way. (Photograph by John Lawson)

RIGHT: An interurban makes its way through traffic on Pasadena's Colorado Street in 1941. (Stephen D. Maguire Collection) BELOW: A P. E. car crosses the Southern Pacific tracks at Alhambra Avenue on the South Pasadena line, which sped commuters to Los Angeles, in 1906. (Craig Rasmussen Collection)

ABOVE: A Pasadena Short Line car rolls on its private right-of-way en route to Los Angeles in 1949, when the trolley era was nearing its end. (Photo by Vernon J. Sappers) BELOW: This P. E. car, used in Pasadena "local" service, is typical of coaches with open-air sections used in the early 1900's.

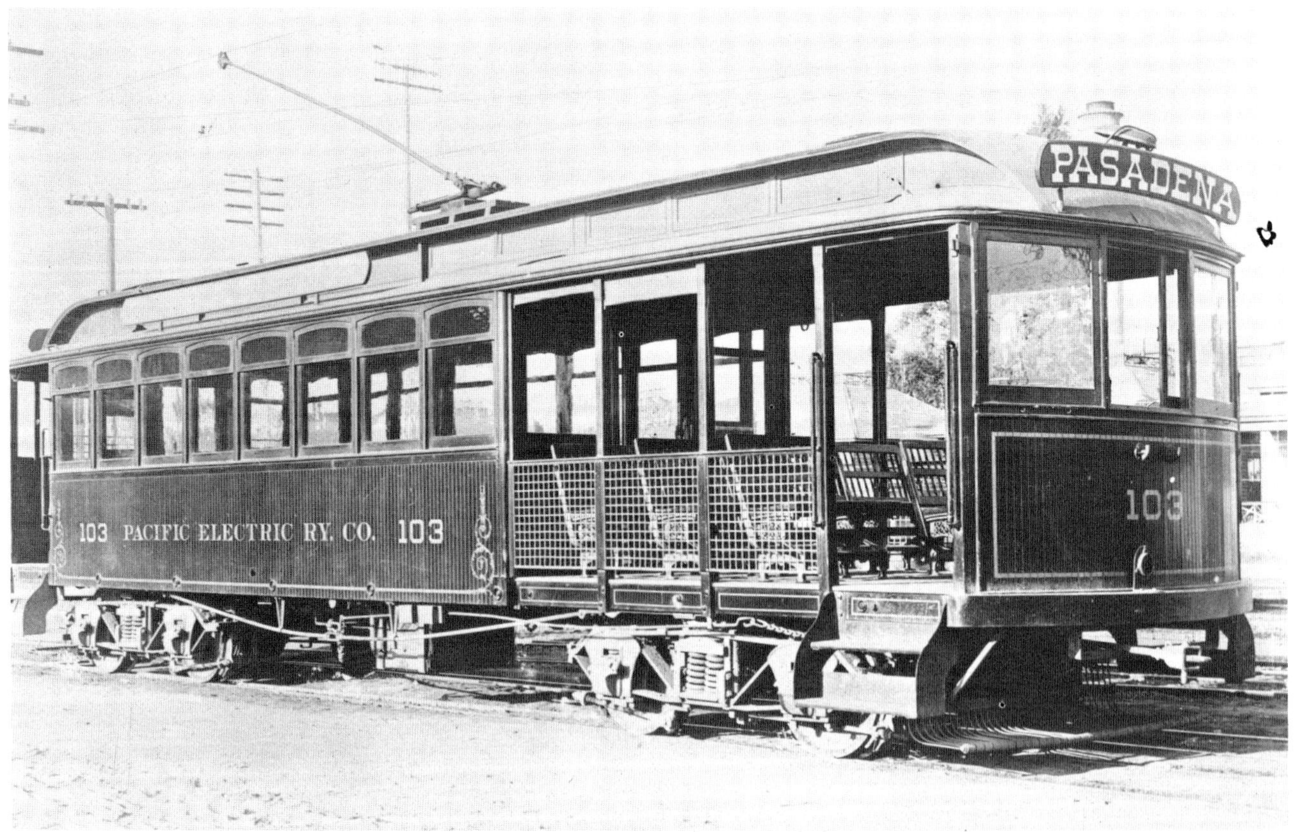

Balloon Route Excursion

The Greatest Moderate Priced Pleasure and Sight Seeing Trip on the Pacific Coast

One Whole Day for One Dollar

101 Miles for 100 Cents

Showing some of California's finest scenery including 28 miles right along the Ocean, through Hollywood, Soldiers' Home, Santa Monica, Ocean Park, Venice, Redondo Beach. Playa del Rey for dinner.

RESERVED SEATS

An Experienced Guide with Each Car

The Only Electric Line Excursion Out of Los Angeles Going One Way and Returning Another

Free Attractions—At Santa Monica, FREE ADMISSION to the CAMERA OBSCURA, an exclusive attraction for Balloon Route Excursionists only. At Venice FREE ADMISSION to the $20,000 Aquarium and a FREE RIDE on the L. A. THOMPSON SCENIC RAILWAY, the longest in the world.

Last Car Leaves Los Angeles

(Hill St. Station Between Fourth and Fifth)

9:40 A. M. DAILY

There were few automobiles or roads in the early twentieth century, but people could enjoy the then-smogless countryside via sightseeing outings on trolleys. Among the most popular tours was the Balloon Route Excursion, which received its name from the shape of the route that took pleased passengers from Los Angeles to Santa Monica and Venice and return. Other tours included the Triangle Trip, going to Santa Ana, Long Beach, and San Pedro; the Old Mission Trolley Trip, stopping at San Gabriel Mission; the Poinsettia Route, covering towns near San Bernardino, and the Orange Empire Trolley Trip, taking sightseers from Los Angeles to the beautiful citrus country around Riverside and San Bernardino. Most tours originally were just $1 per person, although prices increased in the 1920's—a time when popularity of automobiles doomed the trolley tours. BELOW: Large windows and plush seats distinguished this trolley used in 1908 on the Balloon Trip. (Charles Seims Collection)

Southern California Sight-Seeing Trolley Trips

3 PERSONALLY CONDUCTED TOURS TO POINTS OF GREAT INTEREST **3**

Balloon Route Trolley Trip

Visiting all the West Beaches, Hollywood and the Entire Cahuenga Valley with Long Stops at Redondo Beach, Moonstone Beach, the Great Venice of America, Ocean Park and Santa Monica and the National Soldiers' Home.

10 West Coast Beaches, 8 Cities, 28 Miles Along the Ocean

Free Admission to the Camera Obscura, Santa Monica (an Exclusive Attraction), Free Admission to the $20,000 Aquarium, at Venice.

PARLOR CAR SERVICE COMPETENT, COURTEOUS GUIDES

Reserved Seat for Each Patron
Daily from Pacific Electric Station—Last Car 9:30 A. M. $1.00 Pays for All

Old Mission Trolley Trip

Visiting the Orange Groves of the Great San Gabriel Valley, the World's Renowned Cawston Ostrich Farm, Skirting the Foothills of the Great Sierra Madre Mountains—Through the Beautiful San Gabriel Valley—To the "Crown City" Pasadena, Famous Old Mission San Gabriel, and Other Interesting Places. Two hour stop at Pasadena, giving ample time to visit the famous Busch Gardens, Orange Grove Ave., Etc.

Sights and Scenes Not Duplicated in the World

Free admission to the World Famous Cawston Ostrich Farm with its exhibit of live birds and priceless collection of plumes. Free admission to San Gabriel Mission (Established in 1771). Two 25-cent Attractions Free.

$1.00 ONE GREAT DAY AT SIGHTSEEING PARLOR CAR, RESERVED SEAT SERVICE **$1.00**

Daily from Pacific Electric Station, 6th and Main Sts. Last Car, 9:30 A. M.

Triangle Trolley Trip

A trip without a rival, through the heart of Orange County. The great Sugar Beet and Celery Fields; Santa Ana, the hub of the Orange County Agricultural Empire and city of beautiful homes; the New Delhi Sugar Factory; Huntington Beach, Alamitos Bay, Long Beach, the beautiful, and its maze of attractions; San Pedro and the great Los Angeles harbor; the gigantic Government Breakwater; entrancing Point Fermin and its grottoes, cliffs and wild natural nooks amid the swirling spray; a trip ideal, combining commercial and resort attractions.

10 South Coast Beaches, 7 Cities, 30 Miles Along the Ocean

Free admission through the Government Lighthouse Reservation to the outer pinnacle of Point Fermin, from which point a most imposing panorama of nature presents itself.

$1.00 ONE WHOLE DAY OF WHOLESOME PLEASURE PARLOR CAR, GUIDE SERVICE AND RESERVED SEAT **$1.00**

Daily from Pacific Electric Station, 6th and Main Sts. Last Car, 9:30 A. M.
Phones: Main 900, F 2444

LOS ANGELES to REDONDO BEACH via INGLEWOOD and GARDENA—Second Street Station

STATIONS	Mls.	*I	*I	*G	*I	*G	*I	*G	*I	*G	*I	*G	*I	*G	†I	*I	*G	*I	*G	*I	*G	*I	*G	*I	*G	*I	*G	*I
Los Angeles	.0	5 30	6 00	6 20	6 40	7 00	7 20	7 40	8 00	8 20	8 40	9 00	9 20	9 40	9 40	10 00	10 20	10 40	11 00	11 20	11 40	12 00	12 20	12 40	1 00	1 20	1 40	2 00
Inglewood	10.2	6.05	6 35	....	7 15	....	7 55	....	8 35	....	9 15	....	9 55	....	10 15	10 35	....	11 15	....	11 55	....	12 35	....	1 15	....	1 55	....	2 35
Hawthorne	13.2	6 10	6 41	....	7 21	....	8 01	....	8 41	....	9 21	....	10 01	....	10 21	10 41	....	11 21	....	12 01	....	12 41	....	1 21	....	2 01	....	2 41
Lawndale	14.7	6 13	6 44	....	7 24	....	8 04	....	8 44	....	9 24	....	10 04	....	10 24	10 44	....	11 24	....	12 04	....	12 44	....	1 24	....	2 04	....	2 44
Gardena	12.5	....	....	7 01	....	7 41	....	8 21	....	9 01	....	9 41	....	10 21	....	....	11 01	....	11 41	....	12 21	....	1 01	....	1 41	....	2 21	....
Moneta	13.7	....	....	7 04	....	7 44	....	8 24	....	9 04	....	9 44	....	10 24	....	....	11 04	....	11 44	....	12 24	....	1 04	....	1 44	....	2 24	....
Belvidere	16.7	6 16	6 50	7 10	7 30	7 50	8 10	8 30	8 50	9 10	9 30	9 50	10 10	10 30	10 30	10 50	11 10	11 30	11 50	12 10	12 30	12 50	1 10	1 30	1 50	2 10	2 30	2 50
Redondo Beach	20.2	6 23	6 57	7 17	7 37	7 57	8 17	8 37	8 57	9 17	9 37	9 57	10 17	10 37	10 37	10 57	11 17	11 37	11 57	12 17	12 37	12 57	1 17	1 37	1 57	2 17	2 37	2 57
Clifton	22.0	6 28	7 02	7 22	7 42	8 02	8 22	8 42	9 02	9 22	9 42	10 02	10 22	10 42	....	11 02	11 22	[illegible]	[illegible]	[illegible]	[illegible]	[illegible]	[illegible]	[illegible]	[illegible]	[illegible]	[illegible]	[illegible]

STATIONS	Mls.	*G	*I	*G	*I	*G	*I	*G	*I	†S	*G	†FI	*I	*G	*I	*G	*I	*G	*I	*G	*I	*G	*I	*G	*I	*S	*G	S	*I
Los Angeles	.0	2 20	2 40	3 00	3 20	3 40	4 00	4 20	4 40	4 54	5 00	5 10	5 20	5 40	6 00	6 20	6 40	7 00	7 30	8 00	8 30	9 00	9 45	10 30	11 15	11 15	12 00	12 15	12 30
Inglewood	10.2	....	3 15	....	3 55	....	4 35	....	5 15	....	....	5 39	5 55	....	6 35	....	7 15	....	8 02	....	9 02	....	10 17	....	11 47	....	....	....	1 00
Hawthorne	13.2	....	3 21	....	4 01	....	4 41	....	5 21	....	....	....	6 01	....	6 41	....	7 21	....	8 08	....	9 08	....	10 23	....	11 53	....	....	....	1 04
Lawndale	14.7	....	3 24	....	4 04	....	4 44	....	5 24	....	....	....	6 04	....	6 44	....	7 24	....	8 11	....	9 11	....	10 26	....	11 56	....	....	....	1 07
Gardena	12.5	3 01	....	3 41	....	4 21	....	5 01	....	5 36	5 41	....	....	6 21	....	7 01	....	7 41	....	8 38	....	9 38	....	11 08	....	11 55	12 38	12 55	....
Moneta	13.7	3 04	....	3 44	....	4 24	....	5 04	....	5 39	5 44	....	....	6 24	....	7 04	....	7 44	....	8 41	....	9 41	....	11 11	....	11 58	12 41	12 58	....
Belvidere	16.7	3 10	3 30	3 50	4 10	4 30	4 50	5 10	5 30	5 45	5 51	5 50	6 10	6 30	6 50	7 10	7 30	7 50	8 16	8 47	9 16	9 47	10 31	11 17	12 01	12 06	12 47	1 04	1 09
Redondo Beach	20.2	3 17	3 37	3 57	4 17	4 37	4 57	5 17	5 37	5 52	5 57	5 57	6 17	6 37	6 57	7 17	7 37	7 57	8 22	8 53	9 22	9 53	10 37	11 23	12 07	12 12	12 53	1 10	1 15
Clifton	22.0	3 22	3 42	4 02	4 22	4 42	5 02	5 22	5 42	....	6 02	6 02	6 22	6 42	7 02	7 22	7 42	8 02	8 25	9 00	9 25	9 56	10 42	11 28	12 12	12 14	12 58	1 15	1 19

* Daily. † Daily except Sunday. F Flyer. I Via Inglewood. G Via Gardena. S Via Sunnyside. Light figures A. M. Black figures P. M.

REDONDO BEACH via INGLEWOOD

NOTE.—In making the trip to Redondo Beach via Inglewood we advise you to pay the TEN CENTS EXTRA—stop off at Slauson Ave. and see Angeles Mesa. You will find the view of the city from this beautiful plateau the finest to be had. This subdivision of 440 acres is offered in large homesites. ncluding complete high class improvements at from $600 up. Sold on very easy terms. Values absolutely will double in two years. See the agent or call at downtown office—sixth floor—640 South Broadway, Angeles Mesa Land Co.

The Pacific Electric performed a variety of services during its half century in the Los Angeles area. The timetables above shows the frequency of service to Redondo Beach in 1911. RIGHT: This freight express car was operating on the Inglewood line in 1950. (Photograph by Vernon J. Sappers) BELOW: Inland residents took the Big Red Cars to see beach attractions. This is Redondo Beach in 1925. (Security Pacific National Bank Historical Collection)

The region west of Los Angeles also was webbed with convenient P. E. lines. ABOVE: An interurban stops for a passenger on Santa Monica Boulevard in 1919. (Charles Seims Collection) BELOW: Trolleys on the Santa Monica Line used a right-of-way dividing Santa Monica Boulevard in Beverly Hills.

ABOVE: A trolley with center doors stops on Sunset Boulevard by the Beverly Hills Hotel in 1915. (Security Pacific National Bank) RIGHT: P. E. trolleys went along the oceanfront from downtown Santa Monica to Santa Monica Canyon; this photo was made in 1920. (Title Insurance and Trust Co.) LEFT: An electric car waits for passengers at the Santa Monica P. E. station on Ocean near Broadway. (Stephen D. Maguire Collection)

LOS ANGELES - HOLLYWOOD - SANTA MONICA - VENICE LINE

Los Angeles-Hollywood-Beverly Hills-West Los Angeles-Santa Monica-Ocean Park-Venice
Daily Except Sunday Schedule.

LOS ANGELES (Subway Terminal) to VENICE

Lv Los Angeles Subway Terminal via Subway	Lv Hollywood and Western	Ar Beverly Hills	Ar West Los Angeles	Ar Santa Monica	Ar Venice
5.30am	5.50am	6.15am	6.25am	6.37am	6.47am
C 6.00	C 6.20	C 6.45	C 6.59	C 7.12	C-P
6.15	6.35	7.00	7.10	7.22	7.32
C 6.28	C 6.48	C 7.13	C 7.39	C 7.53	C-P
6.55	7.18	7.48	7.58	8.12	8.22
C 7.15	C 7.38	C 8.08	C 8.21	C 8.35	C-P
H 7.09	7.47	8.17	....	....	....
7.36	7.59	8.29	8.39	8.53	9.03
C 7.44	C 8.07	C 8.37	C 8.51	C 9.05	C-P
7.52	8.15	8.45	....	....	....
8.11	8.34	9.04	9.14	9.28	9.38
C 8.35	C 8.58	C 9.28	C 9.41	C 9.55	C-P
8.54	9.17	9.47	9.57	10.11	10.21
C 9.15	C 9.38	C10.08	C10.21	C10.35	C-P
9.35	9.58	10.28	10.38	10.52	11.02
C 9.55	C10.18	C10.48	C11.01	C11.15	C-P
10.15	10.38	11.08	11.18	11.32	11.42
C10.35	C10.58	C11.28	C11.41	C11.55	C-P
10.55	11.18	11.48	11.58	12.12pm	12.22pm
C11.15	C11.38	C12.08pm	C12.21pm	C12.35	C-P
11.35	11.58	12.28	12.38	12.52	1.02
C11.55	C12.18pm	C12.48	C 1.01	C 1.15	C-P
12.15pm	12.38	1.08	1.18	1.32	1.42
C12.35	C12.58	C 1.28	C 1.41	C 1.55	C-P
12.55	1.18	1.48	1.58	2.12	2.22
C 1.15	C 1.38	C 2.08	C 2.21	C 2.35	C-P
1.35	1.58	2.28	2.38	2.52	3.02
C 1.55	C 2.18	C 2.48	C 3.01	C 3.15	C-P
2.15	2.38	3.08	3.18	3.32	3.42
C 2.35	C 2.58	C 3.28	C 3.41	C 3.55	C-P
2.55	3.18	3.48	3.58	4.12	4.22
C 3.15	C 3.39	C 4.09	C 4.24	C 4.38	C-P
3.35	3.59	4.29	4.40	4.54	5.04
C 3.55	C 4.19	C 4.49	C 5.12	C 5.26	C-P
4.12	4.36	5.06	5.17	5.31	5.41
C 4.25	C 4.49	C 5.19	C 5.36	C 5.50	C-P
C 4.35	C 4.59	C 5.29	C 5.48	C 6.02	C-P
4.55	5.19	5.49	6.00	6.14	6.24
C 5.14	C 5.38	C 6.08	C 6.21	C 6.35	C-P
5.36	6.00	6.30	6.41	6.55	7.05
C 5.54	C 6.18	C 6.48	C 7.05	C 7.19	C-P
6.14	6.38	7.08	7.19	7.32	7.42
C 6.24	C 6.47	C 7.16	C 7.29	C 7.42	C-P
6.44	7.07	7.34	7.44	7.57	8.07
C 6.55	C 7.17	C 7.45	C 7.59	C 8.12	C-P
7.18	7.41	8.08	8.18	8.31	8.41
HC 7.12	C 7.47	C 8.14	C 8.29	C 8.42	C-P
HC 7.40	C 8.15	C 8.42	C 8.59	C 9.12	C-P
HC 8.08	C 8.43	C 9.10	C 9.29	C 9.42	C-P
HC 8.38	C 9.13	C 9.40	C 9.59	C10.12	C-P
HC 9.08	C 9.43	C10.10	C10.29	C10.42	C-P
HC 9.38	C10.13	C10.40	C10.59	C11.11	C-P
HC10.08	C10.43	C11.09	C11.29	C11.41	C-P
HC10.38	C11.13	C11.39	C11.59	C12.11am	C-P
HC11.32	C12.03am	C12.28am	C12.39am	C12.51	C-P
AC 1.16	C 1.41	C 2.05	C 2.19	C 2.31	C-P
AW 1.46	W 2.11	....	....	....	....
AW 2.16	W 2.41	....	....	....	....

VENICE to LOS ANGELES (Subway Terminal)

Lv Venice	Lv Ocean Park	Lv Santa Monica	Lv West Los Angeles	Lv Beverly Hills	Ar Hollywood and Western	Ar Los Angeles Subway Terminal via Subway
4.38am	4.43am	4.48am	5.00am	5.10am	5.34am	5.54am
....	T 4.58	T 5.04	T 5.16	5.34	5.59	6.19
....	T 5.32	T 5.38	T 5.50	6.03	6.28	6.48
6.00	6.05	6.10	6.23	6.33	6.59	7.22
....	T 6.11	T 6.17	T 6.30	6.54	7.22	7.45
6.32	6.37	6.42	6.57	7.11	7.42	8.05
....	T 6.59	T 7.05	T 7.19	7.32	8.02	8.25
7.13	7.18	7.23	7.38	7.52	8.23	8.46
....	T 7.38	T 7.44	T 7.58	8.13	8.43	9.06
....	T 7.44	T 7.50	T 8.04	8.23	8.53	9.16
7.55	8.00	8.05	8.20	8.33	9.03	9.26
....	T 8.06	T 8.12	T 8.26	8.43	9.13	9.36
....	T 8.19	T 8.25	T 8.39	8.53	9.23	9.46
8.37	8.42	8.47	9.01	9.13	9.43	10.06
....	T 9.03	T 9.09	T 9.22	9.33	10.03	10.26
9.17	9.22	9.27	9.41	9.53	10.23	10.46
....	T 9.40	T 9.46	T 9.59	10.13	10.43	11.06
9.57	10.02	10.07	10.21	10.33	11.03	11.26
....	T10.20	T10.26	T10.39	10.53	11.23	11.46
10.37	10.42	10.47	11.01	11.13	11.43	12.06pm
....	T11.00	T11.06	T11.19	11.33	12.03pm	12.26
11.17	11.22	11.27	11.41	11.53	12.23	12.46
....	T11.40	T11.46	T11.59	12.13pm	12.43	1.06
11.57	12.02pm	12.07pm	12.21pm	12.33	1.03	1.26
....	T12.20	T12.26	T12.39	12.53	1.23	1.46
12.37pm	12.42	12.47	1.01	1.13	1.43	2.06
....	T 1.00	T 1.06	T 1.19	1.33	2.03	2.26
1.17	1.22	1.27	1.41	1.53	2.23	2.46
....	T 1.40	T 1.46	T 1.59	2.13	2.43	3.06
1.57	2.02	2.07	2.21	2.33	3.03	3.26
....	T 2.20	T 2.26	T 2.39	2.52	3.22	3.46
2.36	2.41	2.46	3.00	3.12	3.42	4.06
....	T 3.00	T 3.06	T 3.19	3.32	4.02	4.26
3.12	3.17	3.22	3.37	3.50	4.21	4.45
....	T 3.40	T 3.46	T 3.59	4.11	4.42	5.06
....	....	....	....	4.21	4.51	5.15
3.55	4.00	4.05	4.19	4.32	5.03	5.27
....	T 4.15	T 4.21	T 4.34	4.55	5.25	S 5.56
4.33	4.38	4.43	4.57	5.10	5.40	6.04
....	T 4.50	T 4.56	T 5.09	5.31	6.01	6.25
5.10	5.15	5.20	5.34	5.47	6.16	6.39
....	T 5.30	T 5.36	T 5.49	6.01	6.30	S 6.55
5.40	5.45	5.50	6.04	6.17	6.46	7.09
....	T 5.55	T 6.01	T 6.14	6.29	6.58	S 7.26
6.06	6.11	6.16	6.30	6.43	7.12	S 7.40
....	T 6.25	T 6.31	T 6.43	7.00	7.27	S 7.55
6.34	6.39	6.44	6.58	7.10	7.37	S 8.05
....	T 6.55	T 7.01	T 7.13	7.30	7.57	S 8.25
....	T 7.25	T 7.31	T 7.43	8.00	8.27	S 8.55
....	T 7.55	T 8.01	T 8.13	8.30	8.57	S 9.25
....	T 8.25	T 8.31	T 8.43	9.00	9.27	S 9.55
....	T 8.55	T 9.01	T 9.13	9.30	9.57	S10.25
....	T 9.25	T 9.31	T 9.43	10.01	10.27	S10.55
....	T 9.55	T10.01	T10.13	10.31	10.57	S11.25
....	T10.25	T10.31	T10.43	11.01	11.27	S11.55
....	T10.55	T11.01	T11.13	11.31	11.56	12.16am
....	T11.35	T11.41	T11.53	12.05am	12.29am	12.49
....	....	....	....	12.35	12.59	A 1.24

BELOW: A Venice Short Line train of three cars leaves Vineyard Junction in 1949. In the background is a "local" service trolleys operating between the junction and San Vicente Boulevard. (Photograph by Vernon J. Sappers)

ABOVE: A train bound for Los Angeles on the Venice Short Line in 1950 nears the Santa Monica Air Line tracks. BELOW: This train of wood-framed cars heads for Venice in 1949, a time when many commuters still relied on the P. E.'s faithful Big Red Cars. (Both Photos by Vernon J. Sappers)

P. E. TROLLEY TRIP

SUCCESSOR TO TILTON'S TROLLEY TRIP

100 Miles for 100 Cents

The best and cheapest way to see

PASADENA AND THE ORANGE GROVES

SAN PEDRO — LOS ANGELES HARBOR

Giving FREE ADMISSION to

CAWSTON OSTRICH FARM

FREE ADMISSION to

SAN GABRIEL MISSION

(Founded 1771)

and a stop of 2 hours at

LONG BEACH

Reserved Chairs Free

SECURE THEM IN ADVANCE

COMPETENT GUIDES

Last Car Leaves Pacific Electric Depot, 6th and Main Streets

9:30 A. M. DAILY

Commuters and sighteers found it easy in the early 1900's to reach Southern California's orange grove areas, then unmarked by subdivisions or freeways, via P. E. interurbans from busy Los Angeles. ABOVE: This interurban on the Orange Empire Trolley Trip paused at the P. E.'s Upland Station in approximately 1916. (Craig Rasmussen Collection) BELOW: An Orange Empire Trolley Trip car has stopped, probably in the late 1910's, so riders can enjoy a stroll. (Charles Seims Collection)

ABOVE: This photo was made of the first interurban to reach Santa Ana when the line opened in 1905. BELOW: A trolley is heading east in Santa Ana's Fourth Street in 1912; the intersection in Main Street, carrying cars to Orange. (Both Photos: First American Title Insurance and Trust Co.)

Frank Nixon, (left) father of President Nixon, posed while employed in 1907 and 1908 as a motorman on the P. E.'s Whittier line. (Nixon Family Collection) BELOW: The P. E. overpass at Spadra Avenue carried a community welcome. The overpass was removed when passenger service ended and Spadra was widened. (First American Title Insurance and Trust Company) OPPOSITE PAGE: The occasion for this photograph was the arrival in 1903 of the first Big Red Car in Monrovia. (Security Pacific National Bank) BELOW: Passengers board an interurban at the Sierra Madre station on Baldwin Avenue in 1906 for an outing. (Pacific Railroad Publications)

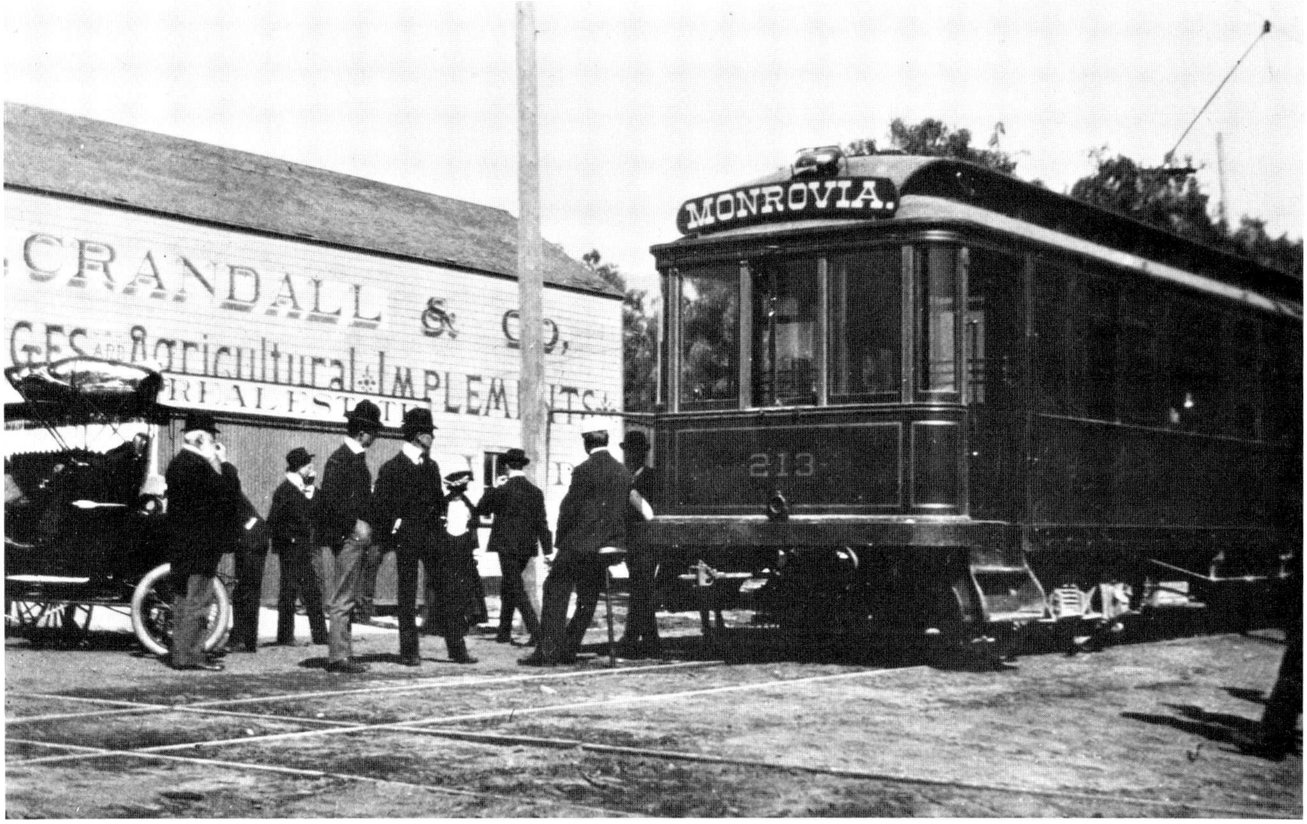
MONROVIA.
CRANDALL & CO.
Agricultural
213

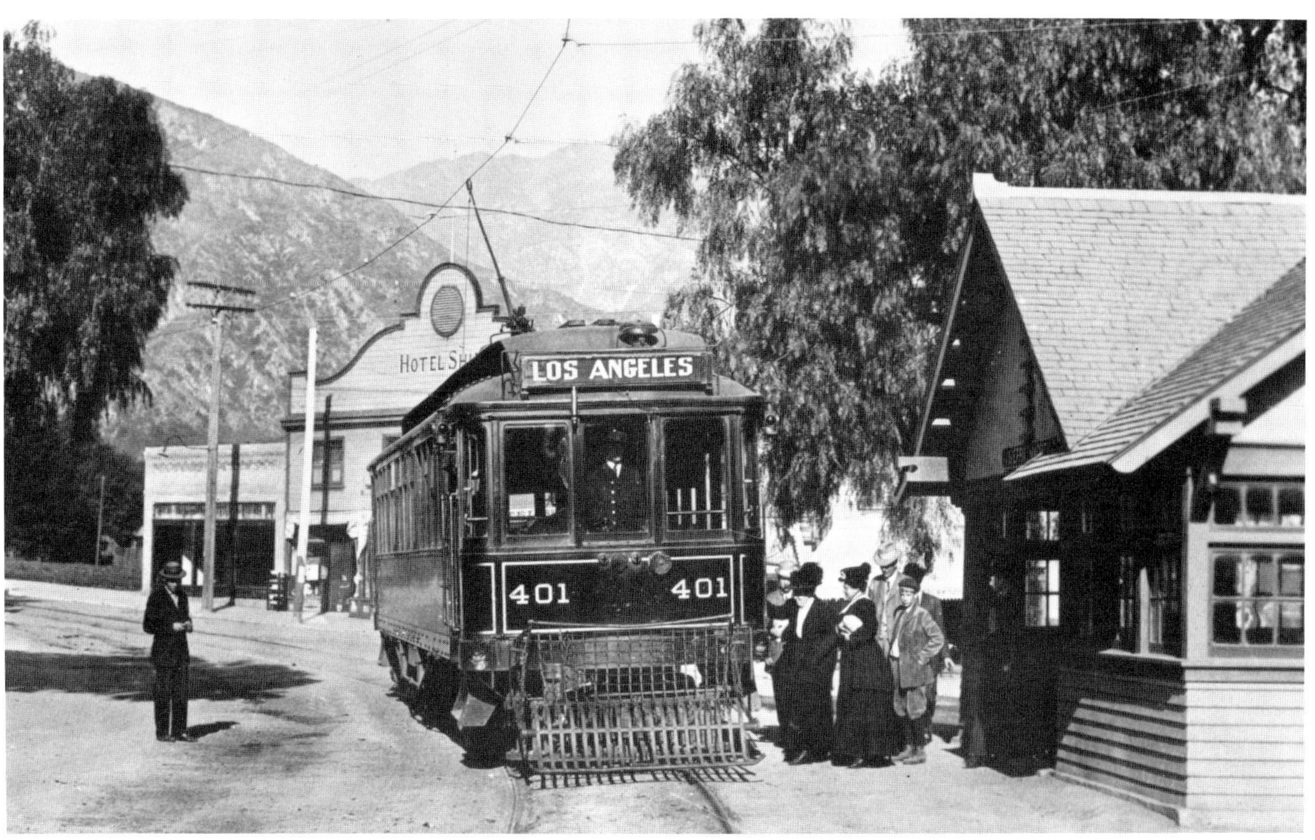

LOS ANGELES
401 401

The 1925 opening of the Hollywood Subway changed routings for many western area lines. Cars entered Glendale Boulevard after leaving the tunnel. LEFT: This drawing shows Glendale-bound cars continuing on Glendale, while Hollywood trolleys go to Sunset Boulevard via Park Avenue. ABOVE: A World War II Subway-bound car was painted to help recruiting. (Photograph by Robert McVay) BELOW: A 1928 view shows the route by Angelus Temple.

ABOVE: A P. E. train travels on Glendale Boulevard past Echo Park Lake, adjoining Angelus Temple. (John Lawson Collection) BELOW: This 1930 photo shows the beautiful Big Red Car route leading to Glendale and Burbank. Commuters relied heavily on the line. (Security Pacific National Bank)

SO. PAC. DEPOT
138

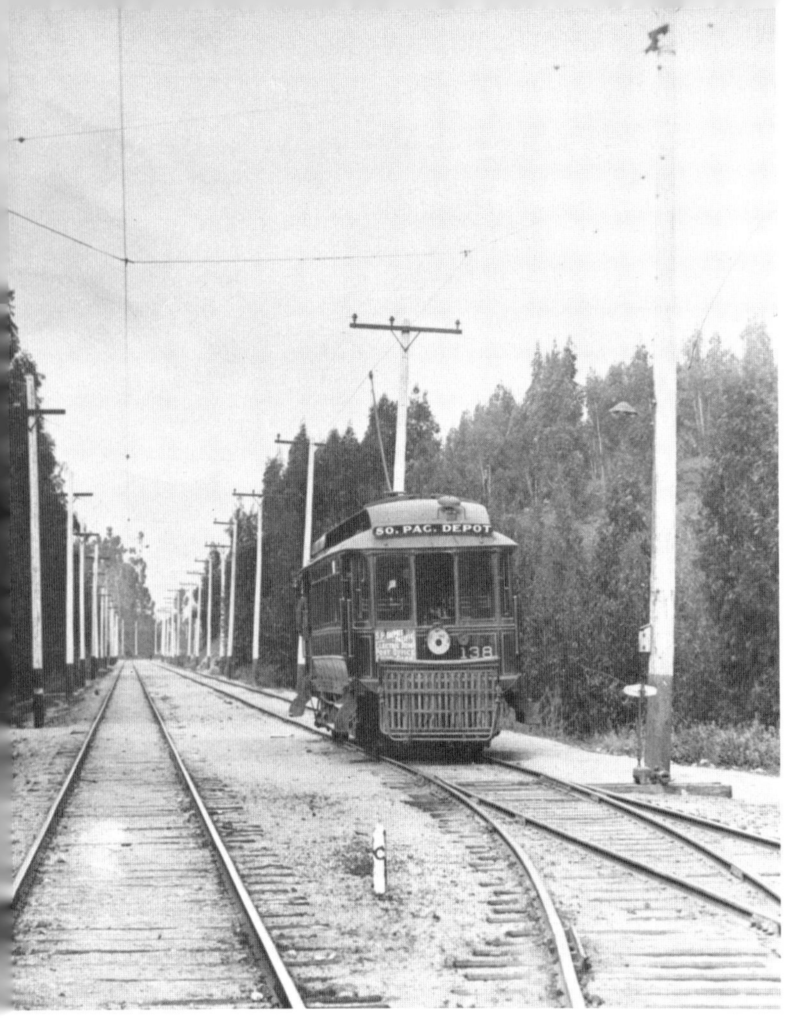

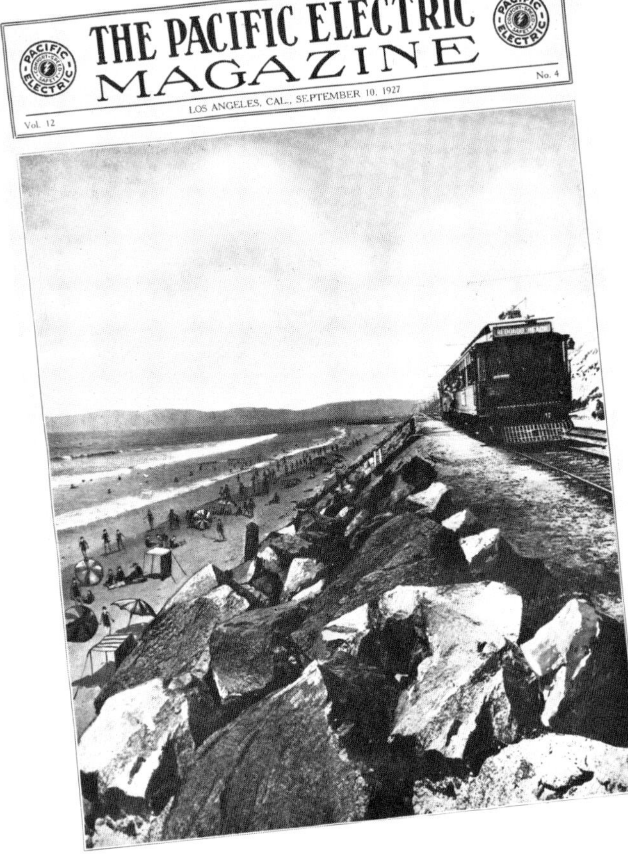

THE PACIFIC ELECTRIC
MAGAZINE
Vol. 12
LOS ANGELES, CAL., SEPTEMBER 10, 1927
No. 4

ABOVE: An interurban in the Glendale route stops at the Semi-Tropical Park terminus of the Edendale line in 1907. ABOVE RIGHT: A 1927 cover of the P. E. Magazine, for employees, featured cars at Manhattan Beach. BELOW: PCC trolleys, most modern cars used by the P. E., went into Glendale-Burbank service in 1940 and provided fast and comfortable service acclaimed by the commuters.

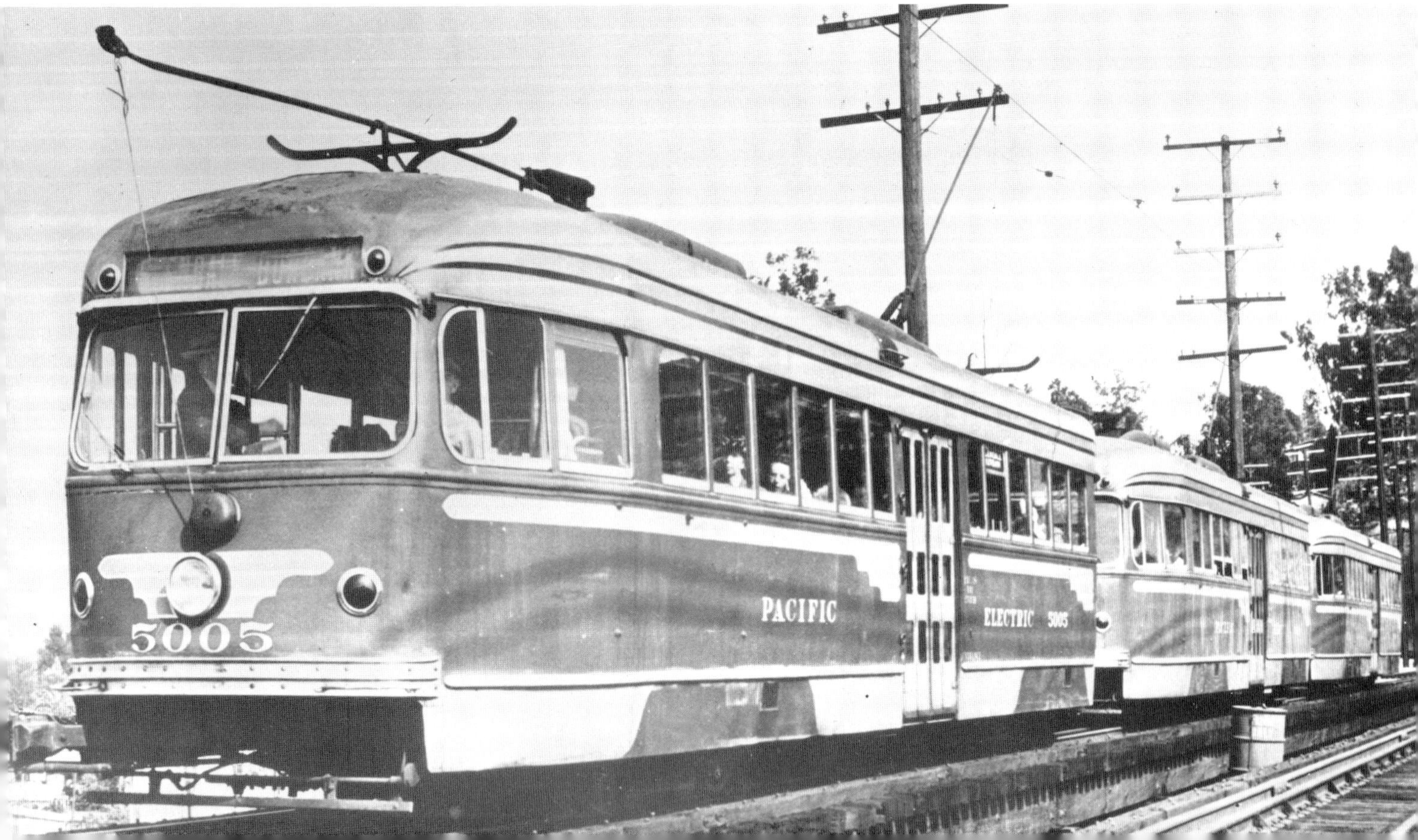
5005
PACIFIC
ELECTRIC 5005

The day is April 8, 1961, last day of service for the Big Red Cars and a train rolls through Compton (right) en route to Long Beach. (Photograph by the Author) The day was nostalgic not only because of the finale for interurbans, but also because at its peak the P. E. network took electric cars frequently and rapidly to beach areas. Commuters could enjoy seaside homes and work in Los Angeles. But best of all for inlanders, the Big Red Cars made it easy to enjoy a variety of beach areas. P. E. cars served Santa Monica, Venice, Playa del Rey, Manhattan Beach, Hermosa Beach, Redondo Beach, San Pedro, Long Beach, Seal Beach, Huntington Beach, Newport Beach, and Balboa. Extra interurbans went into service on holidays and during summers to carry crowds to the beaches. BELOW: This timetable shows typical service during the 1920's from Los Angeles to Newport Beach via Long Beach.

NEWPORT LINE

LOS ANGELES — HUNTINGTON BEACH — NEWPORT BEACH — BALBOA

STATIONS	Miles	*b	*	*	*	*	*	*	*	†b	*	*	*	*	*t
Los Angeles	.00	4 00	6 45	7 45	9 45	11 15	12 45	2 15	3 15	3 19	4 15	5 13	6 15	9 35	12 02
Slauson Jct.	4.27	4 14	6 59	7 59	9 59	11 29	12 59	2 29	3 29	3 33	4 29	5 27	6 29	9 49	12 16
Watts	7.45	4 19	7 04	8 04	10 04	11 34	1 04	2 34	3 34	3 3[illegible]	4 34	5 32	6 35	9 55	12 22
Compton	10.92	4 25	7 10	8 10	10 10	11 40	1 10	2 40	3 40	3 44	4 40	5 3[illegible]	6 41	10 01	12 29
Dominguez Jct.	13.31	4 29	7 14	8 14	10 14	11 44	1 14	2 44	3 44	3 4	4 44	5 42	6 45	10 05	12 34
Willowville	17.52	4 36	7 21	8 21	10 21	11 51	1 21	2 51	3 51	3 55	4 51	5 49	6 52	10 12	12 42
Zaferia	20.11	....	7 27	8 27	10 27	11 57	1 27	2 57	3 57	....	4 57	5 55	6 53	10 18	12 48
Naples	23.60	....	7 31	8 31	10 31	12 01	1 31	3 01	4 01	4 31	5 01	5 59	7 02	10 22	12 52
Seal Beach	24.11	5 18	7 34	8 34	10 34	12 04	1 34	3 04	4 04	4 34	5 04	6 02	7 05	10 25	12 55
Anaheim Landing	24.61	5 19	7 35	8 35	10 35	12 05	1 3[illegible]	3 05	4 05	4 35	5 05	6 03	7 06	10 26	12 56
Sunset Beach	26.70	5 23	7 39	8 39	10 39	12 09	1 39	3 09	4 09	4 39	5 09	6 07	7 11	10 31	1 00
Huntington Beach	32.46	5 35	7 51	8 51	10 51	12 21	1 51	3 21	4 21	4 51	5 22	6 19	7 23	10 43	1 12
Newport Beach	37.82	5 47	8 03	9 03	11 03	12 33	2 03	3 33	4 33	5 03	5 34	6 31	7 35	10 55	1 24
East Newport	38.53	5 49	8 05	9 05	11 05	12 35	2 05	3 35	4 35	5 05	5 36	6 33	7 37	10 57	1 26
Balboa	39.66	5 53	8 09	9 09	11 09	12 39	2 09	3 39	4 39	5 08	5 40	6 37	7 41	11 01	1 30

BALBOA — NEWPORT BEACH — HUNTINGTON BEACH — LOS ANGELES

STATIONS	Miles	*	*	*	*	*	*	*	*	*	*	†b	*	*	*t
Balboa	.00	5 15	6 20	7 02	8 15	9 45	11 15	12 45	2 15	3 45	4 45	5 16	6 00	8 00	11 20
East Newport	1.13	5 19	6 24	7 06	8 19	9 49	11 19	12 49	2 19	3 49	4 49	5 20	6 04	8 04	11 24
Newport Beach	1.84	5 21	6 26	7 08	8 21	9 51	11 21	12 51	2 21	3 51	4 51	5 22	6 06	8 06	11 26
Huntington Beach	7.20	5 33	6 38	7 20	8 33	10 03	11 33	1 03	2 33	4 03	5 03	5 34	6 18	8 18	11 38
Sunset Beach	12.96	5 44	6 49	7 31	8 44	10 14	11 44	1 14	2 44	4 14	5 14	5 45	6 29	8 30	11 45
Anaheim Landing	15.05	5 48	6 53	7 35	8 48	10 18	11 48	1 18	2 48	4 18	5 18	5 49	6 33	8 35	11 50
Seal Beach	15.55	5 49	6 54	7 36	8 49	10 19	11 49	1 19	2 49	4 19	5 19	5 50	6 34	8 36	11 51
Naples	16.66	5 52	6 57	7 39	8 52	10 22	11 52	1 22	2 52	4 22	5 22	5 53	6 37	8 39	11 53
Zaferia	19.53	5 56	7 01	7 43	8 56	10 26	11 56	1 26	2 56	4 26	5 26		6 41	8 43	11 57
Willowville	22.14	6 02	7 07	7 49	9 02	10 32	12 02	1 32	3 02	4 32	5 32	6 17	6 47	8 49	12 06
Dominguez Jct.	26.95	6 09	7 14	7 56	9 09	10 39	12 09	1 39	3 09	4 39	5 39	6 24	6 54	8 56	12 14
Compton	28.74	6 13	7 18	8 00	9 13	10 43	12 13	1 43	3 13	4 43	5 43	6 29	6 58	9 00	12 19
Watts	32.21	6 19	7 24	8 06	9 19	10 49	12 19	1 49	3 19	4 49	5 49	6 36	7 04	9 06	12 26
Slauson Jct.	35.39	6 24	7 29	8 11	9 24	10 54	12 24	1 54	3 24	4 54	5 54	6 42	7 09	9 12	12 32
Los Angeles	39.66	6 38	7 43	8 25	9 38	11 08	12 33	2 08	3 33	5 08	6 08	6 57	7 23	9 27	12 47

* Daily. † Daily except Sunday. b Via Long Beach. t Transfer to and from Long Beach train at Willowville. Newport trains will stop on signal at Slauson Jct., Watts, Compton, Dominguez Jct., Willowville and Zaferia and all stations between Zaferia and Balboa. Light figures A. M. Dark figures P. M.

Mt. Lowe

MILE HIGH

$2.00

Long Beach—Huntington Beach—Newport—Balboa—Santa Ana
Not through, but connecting service

Lv. Lg. Bch.	Lv. Balboa
7 03	5 15r
8 03	6 20
10 03	7 02
11 33	8 15
1 03	9 45
2 33	11 15
3 33	12 45
RPO 4 14	2 15
4 33	3 45
5 23	4 45
6 33	RPO 5 16
8 13	6 00
12 05	8 00
	11 20

All-connections via Seal Beach except as marked. r-via Zaferia.

LONG BEACH—SAN PEDRO

LONG BEACH — Via Direct Line — SAN PEDRO

STATIONS	Miles	*	*	*	*	*	*	*	*	*	*	*	*	*	*	*	*	*	*	*	*	*	*	*
Long Beach, Pine St.	.00	5 55	6 35	7 15	7 55	8 35	9 15	9 55	10 35	11 15	11 55	12 35	1 15	1 55	2 35	3 15	3 55	4 35	5 15	6 05	7 15	8 35	9 55	11 15
East Wilmington	4.00	6 09	6 49	7 29	8 09	8 49	9 29	10 09	10 49	11 29	12 09	12 49	1 29	2 09	2 49	3 29	4 09	4 49	5 29	6 21	7 29	8 49	10 09	11 29
Wilmington, Canal St.	5.20	6 13	6 53	7 33	8 13	8 53	9 33	10 13	10 53	11 33	12 13	12 53	1 33	2 13	2 53	3 33	4 13	4 53	5 33	6 25	7 33	8 53	10 13	11 33
San Pedro, 5th St.	7.82	6 23	7 03	7 43	8 23	9 03	9 43	10 23	11 03	11 43	12 23	1 03	1 43	2 23	3 03	3 43	4 23	5 03	5 43	6 35	7 43	9 03	10 23	11 43

* Daily. Catalina connection 9:15 A. M. daily. Light figures A. M. Dark figures P. M.

SAN PEDRO — LONG BEACH

STATIONS	Miles	*	*	*	*	*	*	*	*	*	*	*	*	*	*	*	*	*	*	*	*	*	*	*
San Pedro, 5th St.	.00	6 40	7 20	8 00	8 40	9 20	10 00	10 40	11 20	12 01	12 40	1 20	2 00	2 40	3 20	4 00	4 40	5 20	6 01	6 40	8 00	9 20	10 40	12 01
Wilmington, Canal St.	2.62	6 50	7 30	8 10	8 50	9 30	10 10	10 50	11 30	12 10	12 50	1 30	2 10	2 50	3 30	4 10	4 50	5 30	6 11	6 50	8 10	9 30	10 50	12 10
East Wilmington	3.82	6 54	7 34	8 14	8 54	9 34	10 14	10 54	11 34	12 14	12 54	1 34	2 14	2 54	3 34	4 14	4 54	5 34	6 15	6 54	8 14	9 34	10 54	12 14
Long Beach, Pine St.	7.82	7 08	7 48	8 28	9 08	9 48	10 28	11 08	11 48	12 28	1 08	1 48	2 28	3 08	3 48	4 28	5 08	5 48	6 29	7 08	8 28	9 48	11 08	12 28

* Daily. Catalina connection 6:01 P. M. daily. Light figures A. M. Dark figures P. M.

LOS ANGELES CATALINA ISLAND

Outbound from Los Angeles	Miles	*	
Los Angeles	.00	9 15	....
San Pedro	22.00	10 00	....
Avalon, C. I.	49.08	12 15	....
Inbound from Avalon	**Miles**	*	
Avalon, C. I.	.00	3 30	....
San Pedro	27.08	5 45	....
Los Angeles	49.08	6 37	....

* Daily. Light figures A. M. Dark figures P. M. For schedule of cars between Los Angeles and San Pedro, see San Pedro via Dominguez line.

A village with only 2,252 residents in 1900, Long Beach boomed when P. E. connections to Los Angeles opened in 1902. New residents arrived via interurbans and by 1910 the city's population had soared to 17,809. This 1910 photo shows Ocean Boulevard looking south from Pine. (Title Insurance and Trust Co.)

LONG BEACH LOCAL LINES

ALAMITOS BAY AND SEASIDE PARK LINE

Cars leave Pine Street for Alamitos Bay at 5:40 A. M., 6:05 A. M. and every 20 minutes until 7:05 P. M.; then 7:30 P. M. and every thirty minutes until 15 M. N. Cars leave Alamitos Bay 6:05 A. M. and every twenty minutes until 7.25 P. M.; then 7:50 P. M. and every thirty minutes until 12.20 A. M.

Cars leave Pine St. for Seaside Park at 5:45 A. M. and every twenty minutes until 7:45 P. M.; then 8:10 P. M. and every thirty minutes until 12.10 A. M. Cars leave Seaside Park at 5:55 A. M. and every twenty minutes until 7:20 P. M.; then every thirty minutes until 12:20 A. M.

WILLOWS LOCAL AND WEST 7th ST. LINE

Cars run on American Ave., Ocean Ave., Pine St. and West 7th St.

Cars leave Willows at 5;40 A. M., 6:05 A. M. and every thirty minutes until 6:35 P. M.; then 7:15 P. M. and every thirty minutes until 12:45 A. M. Cars leave Pine St. Station for Willows 5:25 A. M., 5:50 A. M., 6:20 A. M. 6:45 A. M. and every thirty minutes until 6:45 P. M.; then 7:07 P. M., 7:30 P. M. and every thirty minutes until 12:30 A. M.

Cars leave Pine St. Station for West 7th St. at 5:45 A. M., 6:20 A. M., and every thirty minutes until 6:50 P. M.

Cars leave 7th and Riverside Drive at 6:05 A. M. and every thirty minutes until 6:35 P. M.; then 7:00 P. M.

MAGNOLIA AVE. AND PINE ST. LOOP

Cars run on Ocean Ave., Magnolia Ave., 14th St. and Pine St.

Cars leave Pine St. Station for 14th St. and American Ave. via Ocean and Magnolia Aves. at 6:05 A. M., and every twenty minutes until 6;50 P. M., then 7;30 P.M. and every 30 minutes until 12;00 A. M.

Cars leave 14th St. and American Ave. for Pine St. Station, via Magnolia Ave., at 6.15 A. M. and every twenty minutes until 6:55 P. M., then 7;20 P. M. and every 30 minutes until 12;20 A. M.

Cars leave Pine St. Station for 14th St. and American Ave., via Pine St. at 6:05 A. M. and every twenty minutes until 6:45 P. M., then 7;15 P. M., 7;35 P. M., and every 30 minutes until 12;05 A. M.

Cars leave 14th St. and American Ave. for Pine St. Station, via Pine St., at 6:17 A. M. and every twenty minutes until 11:55 P. M.

EAST 7th ST. AND EAST 1st ST. LOOP

Cars run on Pine St., East 7th St., Redondo Ave. and East 1st St.

Cars leave Pine St. Station for 7th St. and Redondo Ave., via Pine and East 7th St., at 5:50 A. M., and every twenty minutes until 11:50 P. M.

Cars leave 7th St. and Redondo Ave. for Pine St. Station, via East 7th St., at 6:12 A. M. and every twenty minutes until 12:12 A. M.

Cars leave Pine St. Station for 7th and Redondo Ave., via Ocean and Pacific Aves. and East 1st St., 5:50 A. M. and every twenty minutes until 11:50 P. M.

Cars leave 7th St. and Redondo Ave. for Pine St. Station, via East 1st St., at 6:12 A. M. and every twenty minutes until 12:12 A. M.

REDONDO AVE. LINE

Cars run on Pine St., East Third St., Railroad St. and Redondo Ave. First car leaves Pine and Ocean Ave. at 6:00 A. M., and every 20 minutes until 6:40 P. M. Then every 40 minutes until 12:00 midnight. Returning cars leave Zaferia 20 minutes later than time shown out of Pine and Ocean Ave.

NOTE—Cars leaving Pine and Ocean Ave., at 7:40, 9:00, 10:40 A. M.; 12:20, 2:00, 3:20, 5:20, 6:20, 8:00, 11:20 P. M., connect at Zaferia with cars for Newport Beach and Balboa.

ABOVE: P. E. cars operate on Long Beach's Pine Avenue between Ocean Boulevard and First Street in about 1900. (Charles Seims Collection) LEFT: A P. E. schedule noted Long Beach "local" service.

Four tracks were required because traffic was so heavy on the Pacific Electric's "southern corridor" right-of-way from Los Angeles to Watts. This view in the 1950's shows an interurban speeding to Bellflower while a Watts "local" trolley uses another track. (Pacific Railroad Publications Collection)

The Hotel Virginia, at Magnolia and Ocean in Long Beach, was an exclusive hostelry until its demolition in 1933. This early twentieth century scene shows a P. E. tour car that carried guests on guided trips along the coast and into orange groves. (Charles Seims Collection) BELOW: The P. E. operated the Maryland Special, pictured in 1905, to carry vacationers between the Maryland Hotel in Pasadena and the Virginia. Autos were novel and trolleys accepted in this era. (Craig Rasmussen Collection)

SAN PEDRO LOCAL LINES

POINT FIRMIN LINE

Cars run on Sixth St. and Pacific Ave. First car leaves Sixth and Palos Verde at 6:00 A. M. and then every 30 minutes until 10:30 P. M., then 11:30 P. M. First car leaves Point Firmin at 6:15 A. M., and then every 30 minutes until 10:45 P. M., then 12:00 Midnight—last car.

LA RAMBLA LINE

Cars run on Sixth, Fifth and Alameda Sts. First car leaves Sixth and Palos Verde at 6:15 A. M., and hourly until 6:15 P. M. Then 7:00 P. M. and hourly until 11:00 P. M. Returning cars leave La Rambla 15 minutes later than time shown out of Sixth and Palos Verde.

OUTER HARBOR LINE

Cars un on Sixth St., Pacific Ave., Fourteenth St. and San Pedro St. First car leaves Sixth and Palos Verde at 6:45 A. M., then hourly until 5:45 P. M. Returning leave Outer Harbor 15 minutes later than time shown out of Sixth and Palos Verde.

WEST BASIN LINE

Car leaves San Pedro at 2;30 P. M. to the West Basin via the Bay Shore Line, due at Wilmington 2;40 P. M., West Basin 3:00 P. M. Leave Wilmington 3:15 P M. arrive San Pedro 3:25 P. M.

ABOVE: An interurban on the San Pedro via Gardena Line stops for passengers in Gardena in 1938. (Photograph by Vernon J. Sappers) The adjoining excerpt from a 1911 P. E. schedule details San Pedro "local" service. BELOW: A Big Red Car crosses a bridge en route to San Pedro over the high-speed P. E. line during the 1950's. The line also carried freight. (Pacific Railroad Publications)

ABOVE: An interurban going west on First Street turns onto Pine Avenue in Long Beach during the late 1920's. (Security Pacific National Bank) BELOW LEFT: A Big Red Car speeds to Long Beach on its right-of-way after leaving Dominguez Junction. (Pacific Railroad Publications) BELOW RIGHT: An East Seventh Street "local" Birney trolley waits by the Long Beach library at Pacific and Ocean.

Interurbans rolling down the high-speed P. E. right-of-way from Los Angeles through Watts and Compton served a variety of needs through the years. RIGHT: These cars were photographed at the Catalina Island Terminal on December 7, 1958, last day of trolley service to the facility. "Specials" carried passengers for years to the ships. (Stephen D. Maguire Collection) CENTER: This group posed for a picture at Huntington Beach in 1909 as a momento of the guided Triangle Trolley Trip. (Craig Rasmussen Collection) BELOW RIGHT: The popularity of the Big Red Cars never waned with the years. This crowd in 1956 was celebrating the 50th anniversary of completion of the line to Huntington Beach. (Photograph by Forrest Kimmler)

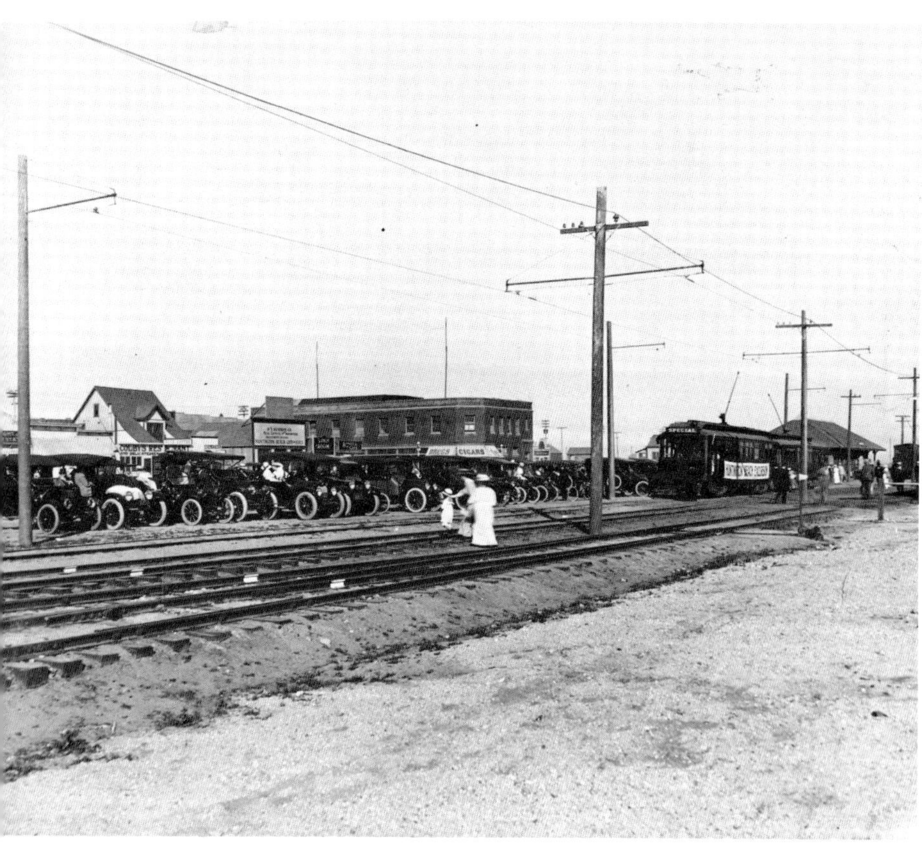

When Henry E. Huntington began building his trolley empire, he also bought large land holdings; values skyrocketed when interurbans made the properties easy for commuters to reach. Among his acquisitions was Pacific City. He changed the village's name to Huntington Beach and his interurban line there opened in June, 1904. The city began to grow. TOP: Here is Huntington Beach in 1915, looking toward the pier at the foot of Main Street. (Author's Collection) LEFT: This photo of the same era shows an excursion car waiting for sightseers to return. (First American Title Insurance and Trust Co.) TOP RIGHT: This car rushed freight to Huntington Beach in the early twentieth century. BOTTOM: A 2-car Catalina Special picks up speed as it goes to meet the island steamer. (Pacific Railroad Publications)

HUNTINGTON BEACH
607
BAGGAGE
EXPRESS.
607
PACIFIC ELECTRIC
OMPA

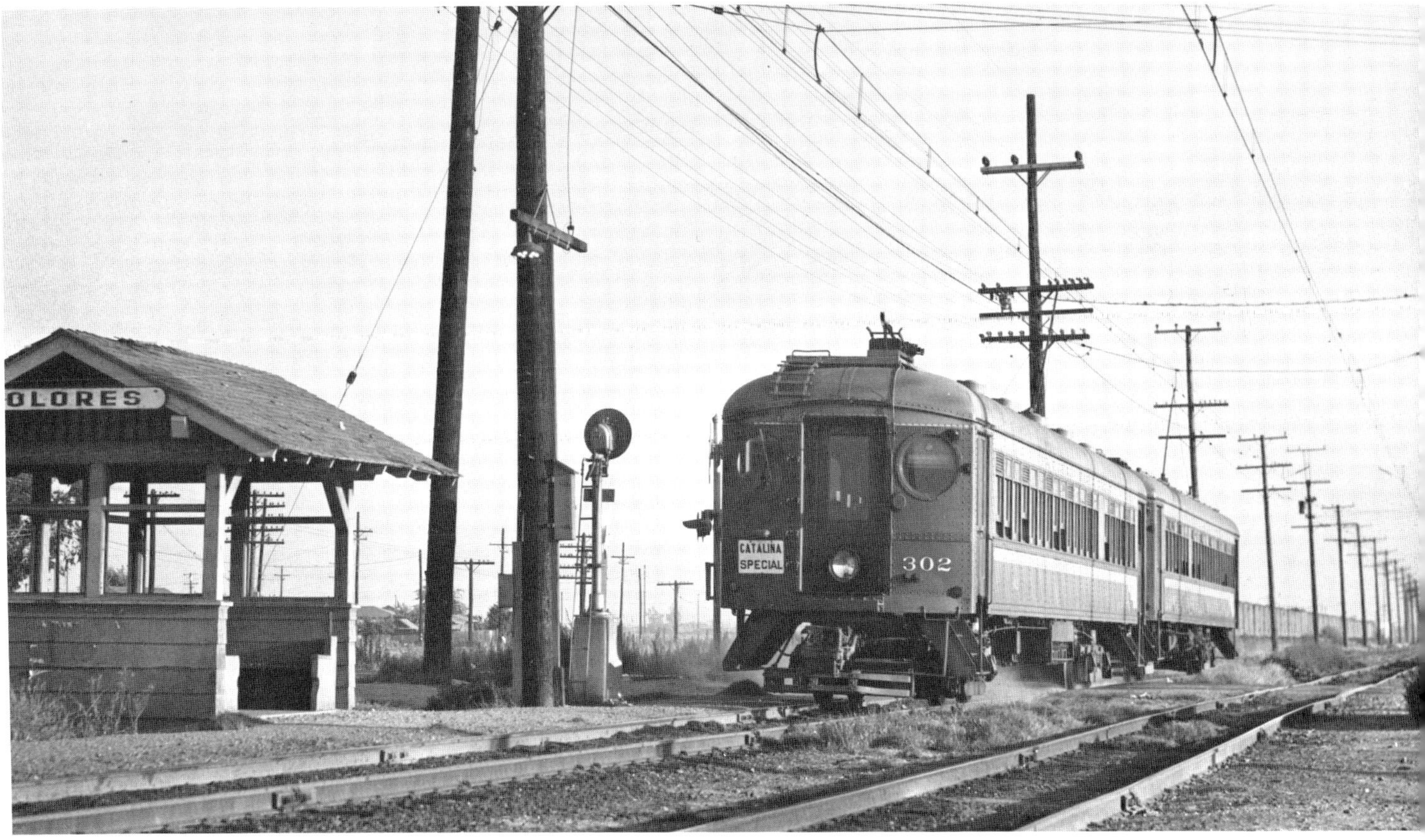
OLORES
CATALINA
SPECIAL
302

ABOVE: This car serving the San Pedro via Gardena Line stands at San Pedro in 1938. Top of the P. E. station is visible in the right background. (Photo by Vernon J. Sappers) BELOW: Cars linking Long Beach and San Pedro wait on Ocean between Pacific and Pine in Long Beach. (Photo by Maxine Reams)

An interurban bound for San Pedro turns onto Pacific from Ocean Boulevard in 1930. Behind it is a Birney trolley (with one man serving as conductor and motorman) serving the East Seventh Street Line. The P. E. station was on the opposite side of Ocean Boulevard. (Security Pacific National Bank Collection)

ABOVE: A 3-car train, en route to San Pedro in the 1950's, was headed by a unit divided for passengers and express. (Pacific Railroad Publications) BELOW: After completing runs in the Long Beach area, cars were serviced in the Morgan Yards, adjacent to the Los Angeles River. (Photo by Maxine Reams)

The Big Red Cars came in many shapes and sizes during the years. ABOVE: A 1904 view shows an interurban that provided Railway Post Office quarters. (Craig Rasmussen Collection) CENTER: Slow and bulky, this trolley did "local" service in Pasadena. BOTTOM: This interurban operated between San Bernardino and Arrowhead Hot Springs. (Both Photos: Stephen D. Maguire Collection)

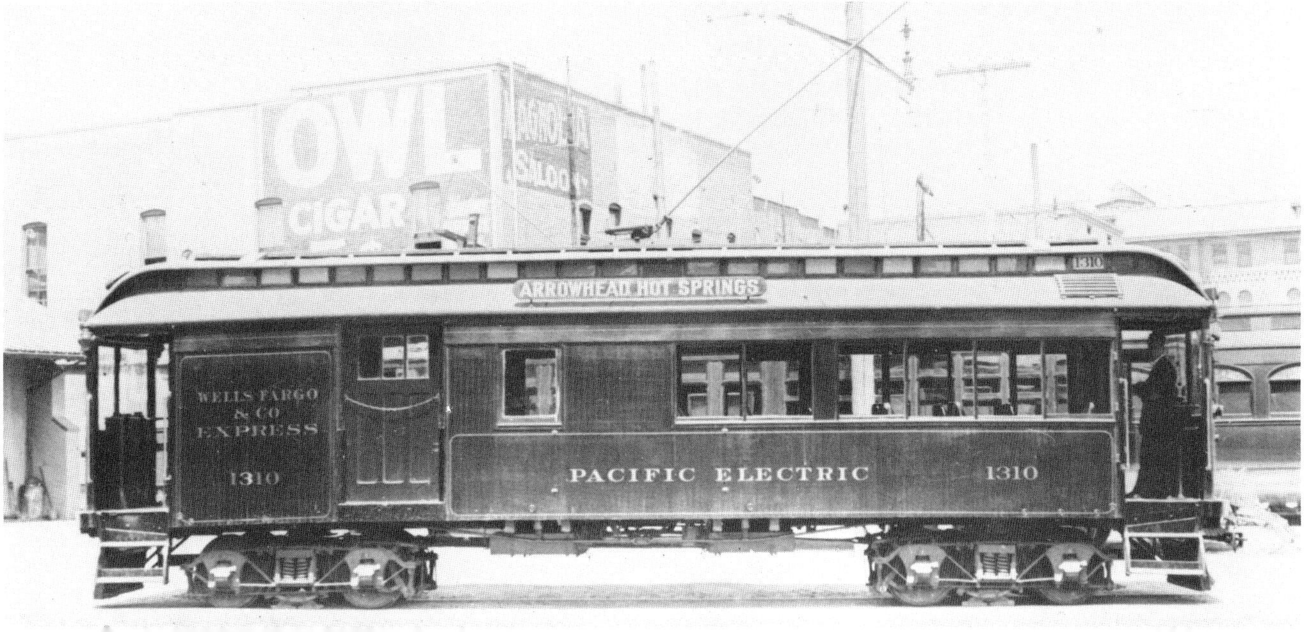

ABOVE: These Big Red Cars were "parked" in the P. E. yard at Venice in April, 1950, while awaiting rush hour duty. (Photograph by Vernon J. Sappers) BELOW LEFT: Here is the trim interior of a typical P. E. car. (Pacific Electric) BELOW RIGHT: Craftsman adjust a trolley at the Long Beach yards. P. E. yards and car barns were situated at key points on the system. (Photo by Maxine Reams)

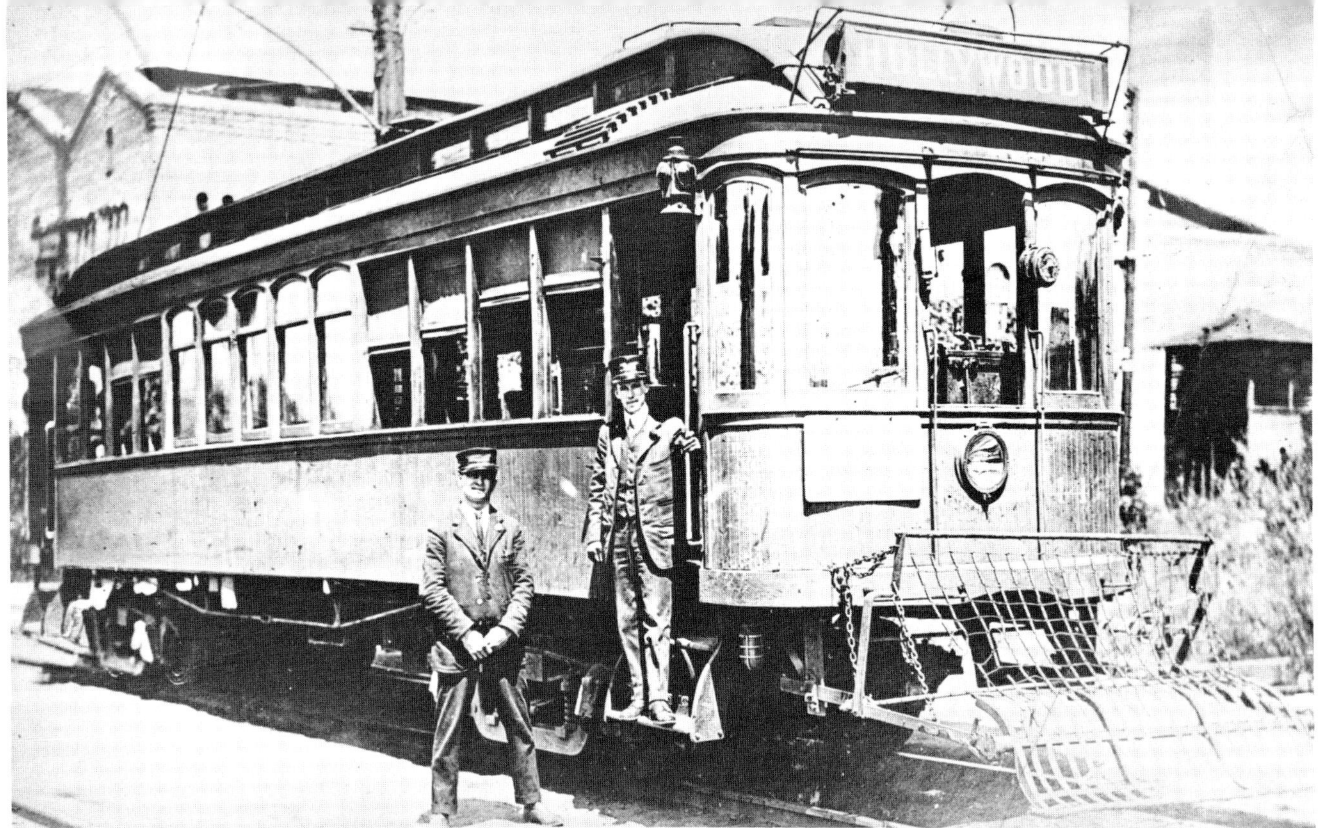

Boasting an open end for aficionados of fresh air, this Los Angeles Pacific trolley was photographed at Highland Avenue in Hollywood in the early 1900's. (Stephen D. Maguire Collection)

THE APPENDIX: Where the Trolleys Ran

The major interurban lines operated by the Pacific Electric are listed here, along with the details, when available, of (1) where the tracks were situated; (2) mileages between points; (3) frequency of service, and (4) running times between major stations.

For most of the first half of the twentieth century, the Big Red Cars, along with their tracks and schedules, were among the most familiar of things to Southern Californians. With the departure of the trolleys, however, it became virtually impossible to determine the routes or other data without accurate records.

The author has compiled this information for those not familiar with the system, but who may wish to retrace the routes and schedules followed by the Red Cars. It must be emphasized that some routes were combined or used in part to form other lines over the years; the compilations here represent only the major lines of the Pacific Electric. Note also should be made that changes in residential developments and work patterns also varied running times and the relative importance of various lines.

The Pacific Electric's main enemy was the automobile, which attacked the trolley system in two major ways. Automobiles cut across rights-of-way and crowded streets once dominated by electric cars, slowing schedules. The increasing number of automobiles also resulted in better roads, which carried commuters faster and more directly between their homes and places of employment. The technology of the automobile and its highways progressed fantastically from 1900 to 1950. Only minor changes were made in the technology of the electric cars during these years; virtually no improvements were made in railroad right-of-ways.

The distance between points on the lines are based on official Pacific Electric timetables and other records. The frequency of schedules and representative running times also were obtained from timetables and have been included to show how people traveled when the Pacific Electric served the Los Angeles area.

In regard to running times, it should be noted that those from 1925 onward usually represent *scheduled* travel time rather than *actual* timing. The increasing volume of automobile traffic starting in the 1920's played a great role in slowing the electric cars.

A two-car Pacific Electric train rolls up the high-speed Long Beach Los Angeles rail artery in the late 1940's. Roads cutting into the right-of-way slowed cars. (Pacific Railway Publications)

SOUTHERN DISTRICT

The Pacific Electric's Southern District embraced all of the lines in Orange County, plus those in southeastern Los Angeles County. For the purpose of these listings, the author has divided the lines into those connected to Los Angeles by the southern "corridor," and those operating between district cities.

Southern "Corridor" Route

The lines of the Pacific Electric Southern District connected to Los Angeles followed a common route to Slauson Junction. Use of the route began July 4, 1902, with opening of the Long Beach Line. At that time the tracks went from Sixth and Main Streets in Los Angeles east on Ninth (which became Olympic Boulevard in the 1,000 block) to Tennessee Street (later renamed Hooper Street), and then turned south onto a private right-of-way. After opening of the elevated tracks from the Pacific Electric Building at Sixth and Main in 1910, the route was on these tracks to San Pedro Street, and south on San Pedro to Ninth, where it connected to Hooper. The private right-of-way from this point divided Long Beach Avenue to Slauson Junction, situated one block south of Slauson Avenue.

MILEAGES:

Los Angeles	0.00
Slauson Junction	4.27

LONG BEACH LINE

Passenger service on the Long Beach Line began July 4, 1902, and ended April 8, 1961. *Route:* the line followed the Southern "Corridor" Route to Slauson Junction and from there went south on a private right-of-way through Watts. This right-of-way divided Willowbrook Avenue from 108th Street in Watts to Greenleaf Drive in Compton, continued south through Dominguez Junction (at approximately Alameda Street and Santa Fe Avenue), crossed the Los Angeles River via a private bridge, and in Long Beach at Willow Street ("North Long Beach") divided American Avenue (later renamed Long Beach Boulevard) to Anaheim Street. From Anaheim, the tracks continued in American to Ocean Boulevard, and west on Ocean to P. E. storage yards adjacent to the Los Angeles River at Ocean Boulevard and Loma Vista Drive. There were P. E. car barns on the east side of American between Fifth and Sixth Streets until the late 1910's, and a depot on the south side of Ocean at Pacific until 1961.

MILEAGES:

Slauson Junction	4.27
Watts	7.45
Willowbrook	9.39
Compton	10.92
Dominguez Junction	13.31
Cota	14.96
North Long Beach (Willow Street)	17.52
Long Beach (Pacific and Ocean)	20.37

FREQUENCY OF SERVICE — 1911: every 30 minutes (54 round trips daily); 1920: every 20 minutes; 1934: every 30 minutes; 1946: every 15 minutes between 8 a.m. and 8:30 p.m.

RUNNING TIME — 1911: 40 minutes on locals and 36 minutes on limiteds; 1913: 48 minutes outbound and 50 minutes inbound for locals and 42 minutes outbound and 46 minutes inbound for limiteds; 1926: 51 minutes for limiteds; 1944: 54 minutes for limiteds; 1954: 60 minutes for limiteds.

SAN PEDRO VIA DOMINGUEZ LINE

Passenger service on the San Pedro via Dominguez Line began November 24, 1904, to Wilmington and on July 5, 1905, to San Pedro. *Route:* the line followed the one to Long Beach to Dominguez Junction, where the tracks turned southwesterly on a private right-of-way adjacent to Alameda Street, continuing to Lomita Boulevard; from here, the private right-of-way cut south diagonally, paralleling Drumm Avenue between Cruces and Young Streets. From "B" Street and Island Avenue the private right-of-way paralleled portions of Neptune Avenue and then entered San Pedro on a right-of-way adjacent to Front Street to Harbor Boulevard and then parallel to Harbor Boulevard. The depot was on the east side of Harbor at Fifth Street.

MILEAGES:

Dominguez Junction	13.31
Watson	17.19
Wilmington (Canal Street)	20.06
San Pedro (5th Street)	22.68

FREQUENCY OF SERVICE — 1911: every 30 to 60 minutes (23 round trips daily); 1946: every 20 to 30 minutes (approximately 55 round trips daily).

RUNNING TIME — 1911: 40 minutes to Wilmington and 45 minutes to San Pedro; 1946: approximately 60 minutes to Wilmington and 70 minutes to San Pedro.

HUNTINGTON BEACH-BALBOA LINE

Passenger service started July 4, 1904, to Huntington Beach, August 5, 1905, to Newport Beach, and July 4, 1906, to Balboa. Passenger service ended June 9, 1940, to Balboa, and on June 30, 1950, to Huntington Beach and Newport Beach. *Route:* the line followed the one to Long Beach to approximately a block north of Willow Street, where at 27th Street and Long Beach Boulevard the tracks cut southeasterly over a private right-of-way forming the boundary from Olive Avenue to Pacific Coast Highway between the cities of Long Beach and Signal Hill.

This right-of-way paralleled Appian Way (by the Marine Stadium) from Nieto Avenue to the San Gabriel River in Long Beach, and used private bridges to cross Alamitos Bay and the river. The right-of-way through Seal Beach (originally known as Bay City) was in the center of Electric Avenue and, until 1942, across Anaheim Bay to Sunset Beach. In 1942, construction of the U. S. Naval Ammunition and Net Depot caused the line to be re-routed from Electric Avenue at Seventeenth Street north to Coast Highway. The tracks followed a private right-of-way south of Coast Highway to Phillips Street and then turned onto a private right-of-way dividing Pacific Avenue in Sunset Beach. After leaving this community, the line followed a private right-of-way between Coast Highway and the ocean to the Pacific Electric station on the south side of Ocean Avenue at Main Street in Huntington Beach. From here, the line continued on a private right-of-way south of Coast Highway to approximately Fifty-ninth Street in Newport Beach, where the line entered a private right-of-way dividing Seashore Drive. At Thirty-second Street the tracks curved to Newport Boulevard and at McFadden Place entered a private right-of-way dividing Balboa Boulevard. It continued on Balboa to the line's terminus at Main Street.

MILEAGES:	
North Long Beach (Willow Street)	17.52
Zaferia	20.11
Naples	23.00
Bay City (Seal Beach)	24.11
Anaheim Landing	24.83
Sunset Beach	26.70
Huntington Beach	32.46
Newport Beach	37.82
East Newport	39.66
Balboa	40.00

FREQUENCY OF SERVICE — 1911: approximately every 60 minutes (19 round trips daily; 1940: 9 round trips daily.

RUNNING TIME — 1911: 47 minutes to Seal Beach (Bay City), 62 minutes to Huntington Beach; 74 minutes to Newport Beach, and 80 minutes to Balboa.

SANTA ANA LINE

Passenger service to Santa Ana began November 6, 1905, and was discontinued to points between Bellflower and Santa Ana on July 2, 1950, and to Bellflower on May 25, 1958. *Route:* the line followed the one to Long Beach to Watts, where it cut southeasterly over a private right-of-way dividing Santa Ana Boulevard to Mona Boulevard and dividing Fernwood Avenue (a continuation of Santa Ana) in Lynwood to Wright Road. The tracks then continued on a private right-of-way southeasterly, cutting diagonally through Clearwater (later renamed Paramount) and dividing Flora Vista Street in Bellflower (originally called Somerset). The Pacific Electric station was at the northeast corner of Bellflower Boulevard and Flora Vista in Bellflower. The private right-of-way continued through Artesia (later renamed Dairy Valley), Cypress, Stanton, and Garden Grove. The tracks paralleled the northern boundary of Willowick Golf Course, crossed the Santa Ana River, and then turned eastward, emerging at Artesia Street from the private right-of-way onto Fourth Street in Santa Ana. The tracks continued down Fourth to the Pacific Electric station at 424 East Fourth Street.

MILEAGES:	
Watts	7.45
Lynwood	9.70
Clearwater (Paramount)	13.06
Somerset (Bellflower)	15.40
Artesia	18.43
Cypress	21.65
Stanton	24.69
Benedict	24.77
Garden Grove	28.51
Santa Ana	34.00

FREQUENCY OF SERVICE — 1911: every 30 to 55 minutes (20 round trips daily); 1935: 9 round trips daily; 1940: 13 round trips daily; 1946: 22 round trips daily.

RUNNING TIME — 1911: 34 minutes to Bellflower, 61 minutes to Garden Grove, and 75 minutes to Santa Ana; 1941: 83 minutes to Santa Ana; 1943: 50 minutes to Bellflower, 78 minutes to Garden Grove, and 96 minutes to Santa Ana; 1946: 97 minutes to Santa Ana.

WHITTIER LINE

Passenger service to Whittier began November 7, 1903, and was discontinued south of Walker on January 22, 1938, and over the remainder of the line on March 6, 1938. *Route:* the line followed the one to Long Beach to Slauson Junction, where it turned east in a private right-of-way dividing Randolph Street in Huntington Park. After leaving Randolph Street at Greenwood Avenue in Downey, the private right-of-way continued in a southeasterly direction to Los Nietos, where shortly after crossing Norwalk Boulevard it turned northward. The right-of-way was approximately midway between Gretna and Lynalan Avenues from approximately Mines Boulevard to Whittier Boulevard. The tracks then turned onto Whittier, continuing to Philadelphia Avenue, and went down Philadelphia to the Southern Pacific-Pacific Electric station at Comstock Avenue. The tracks continued one block eastward to Greenleaf Avenue.

MILEAGES:	
Slauson Junction	4.27
Huntington Park	5.42
Maywood Avenue	6.73
Bell	7.19
Baker	7.66
Laguna	10.07
Rio Hondo	11.40
Rivera	12.39
Los Nietos	14.50
State School	16.68
Whittier	17.35

FREQUENCY OF SERVICE — 1911: every 15 to 60 minutes (33 outbound and 31 inbound trips daily); 1935: 1 round trip daily.

RUNNING TIME — 1911: 16 minutes to Huntington Park, 31 minutes to Rivera, 35 minutes to Los Nietos, and 47 minutes to Whittier.

LA HABRA-YORBA LINDA LINE

Passenger service began in 1906 to La Habra and in 1911 to Yorba Linda. *Route:* the line followed the one to Whittier to Los Nietos, from where the private right-of-way continued paralleling Lambert Road from approximately Hommage Avenue to Leffingwell Road, and the Union Pacific right-of-way from approximately Mills Avenue to Walnut Street in La Habra. The Pacific Electric station was between Second and Electric Avenue at Hiatt Street. The tracks paralleled Superior Avenue between Alpine and Fonda Streets. The private right-of-way went southeasterly to Puente Street in Brea, and then headed easterly. The Pacific Electric station was at the right-of-way's intersection with Pomona Avenue. After leaving Brea, the right-of-way turned southeasterly and shortly after crossing Valencia Avenue paralleled the south side of Imperial Highway to Lemon Drive in Yorba Linda. The right-of-way paralleled Park Drive to Yorba Linda Boulevard and ended at Lakeview Avenue.

MILEAGES:	
Los Nietos	14.50
Leffingwell	19.39
Des Moines	20.92
La Habra	22.19
Randolph (Brea)	25.00
Oleo	26.00
Loftus	27.20
Yorba Linda	29.75

FREQUENCY OF SERVICE — 1911: 7 trains daily.

RUNNING TIME — 1911: 14 minutes to Huntington Park, 27 minutes to Rivera, 30 minutes to Los Nietos, 48 minutes to La Habra, and 66 minutes to Yorba Linda.

FULLERTON LINE

Passenger service to Fullerton started in 1917 and ended on January 22, 1938. *Route:* the line followed the one to La Habra and after leaving the Pacific Electric

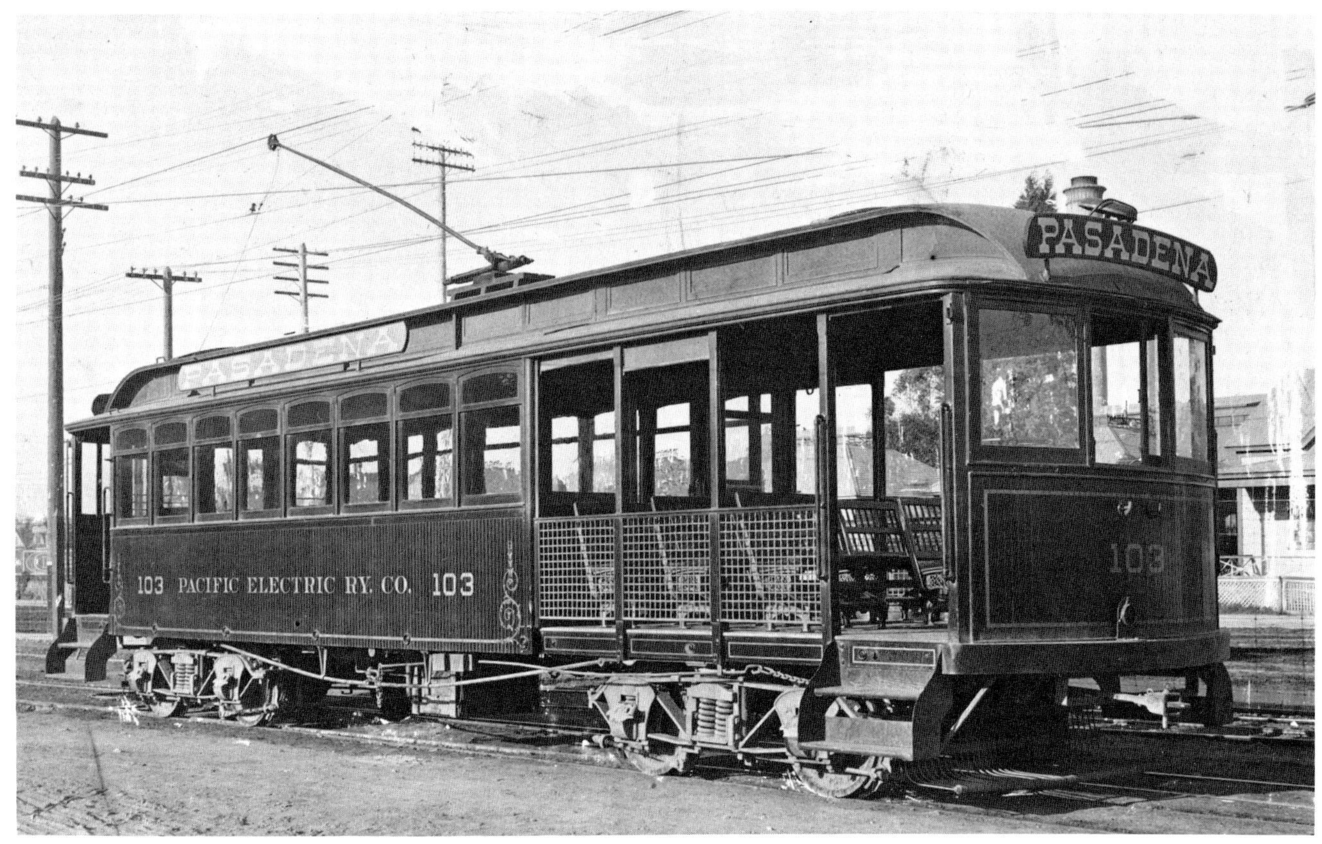

Wooden sides and an open-air section gave beauty to this interurban, which provided "rapid transit" service between Los Angeles and Pasadena in the 1900's. (Stephen D. Maguire Collection)

station there continued on Electric Avenue to Laon Junction (at approximately Bright Avenue). The line then went southward on a private right-of-way which at approximately Valley View Drive turned eastward and crossed Spadra Avenue via an overpass between Hillcrest Park and Glenwood Avenue. The private right-of-way continued east to Harvard Avenue and then curved south, cutting throught what became Fullerton College and south of Chapman Avenue paralleling Lawrence Avenue to Santa Fe Avenue. The private right-of-way paralleled Santa Fe to Pomona Avenue, crossed Pomona, and ended at the Pacific Electric station on the south side of Commonwealth Avenue between Spadra Road and Pomona Avenue.

MILEAGES:

La Habra	22.19
Laon Junction	22.54
Bastanchury	25.11
Sunny Hills	25.22
Fullerton	27.60

FREQUENCY OF SERVICE — 1917: 9 round trips daily; 1937: 1 round trip daily.

RUNNING TIME — 1917: 74 minutes.

REDONDO BEACH VIA GARDENA LINE

Passenger service on this line began November 12, 1911, and ended January 15, 1940. *Route:* the line followed the one to Long Beach to Watts, from where the track headed southwesterly over a private right-of-way paralleling 110th Street from Compton Avenue to Central Avenue, and Lanzit Avenue from Central Avenue to Broadway. The tracks curved southward in a private right-of-way dividing Athens Way to approximately 134th Street and continued south, curving southwesterly and paralleling 149th Street from approximately Figueroa Street to Orchard Street and continuing to Vermont Street. At approximately Compton Boulevard, the private right-of-way turned south and divided Vermont, continuing to Gardena Boulevard where it curved onto 166th Street, dividing 166th from Berendo Avenue to approximately Raymond Avenue. The private right-of-way turned southward approximately one block and headed eastward, paralleling 168th Street. The tracks entered Redondo Beach on Diamond Street. The tracks paralleled the ocean to Clifton.

MILEAGES:

Watts	7.45
South Los Angeles	9.88
Athens	10.31
Strawberry Park	12.75
Gardena	13.57
Hermosillo	14.13
Moneta	14.74
El Nido	17.84
Redondo Beach	20.89
Clifton	22.26

FREQUENCY OF SERVICE — 1911: every 30 minutes (27 round trips daily); 1927: 17 round trips daily.

RUNNING TIME — 1911: 62 minutes; 1922: 64 minutes.

SAN PEDRO VIA TORRANCE LINE

Passenger service began on March 19, 1912, and ended January 15, 1940. *Route:* the line followed the one to Redondo Beach via Gardena to Hermosillo (approximately 166th Street and Raymond Avenue), and followed a private right-of-way curving south to Normandie and then dividing Normandie from approximately 170th Street to 226th Streets.

Tracks left the main route at Dolanco Junction (204th Street) and in a private right-of-way dividing Torrance Boulevard to 212th Street went to the Pacific Electric shops in Torrance. The tracks returned to the main line near 226th Street via Plaza del Amo. From 226th Street, the tracks paralleled Normandie Avenue until just before reaching Leonardo Avenue, where the private right-of-way curved southeasterly across Normandie Avenue and Anaheim Street. The private right-of-way went south adjacent to Gaffey Street to Pacific Avenue, and on Pacific to Front Street. The private right-of-way continued until again meeting Front Street, and the tracks then went on Front to First Street in San Pedro. From here, the tracks followed a private right-of-way adjacent to Front Street to First Street, and parallel to Harbor Boulevard from First Street to Fifth Street.

MILEAGES:

Hermosillo	14.70
Humphreys	16.90
Torrance (Ocean Ave.)	18.90
Weston Street	20.40
San Pedro	25.10

FREQUENCY OF SERVICE — 1922: every 60 minutes; 1934: every 70 minutes.
RUNNING TIME — 1922: 76 minutes outbound and 73 minutes inbound.

EL SEGUNDO LINE

Passenger service to El Segundo began August 10, 1914, and ended October 31, 1930. *Route:* the line followed the one to Redondo via Gardena to South Los Angeles, where at 116th Place and Broadway the private right-of-way continued eastward midway between 116th and 117th Streets to Vermont Avenue. From here, the private right-of-way went southeasterly parallelling Broadway from Crenshaw Boulevard to Inglewood Avenue in Hawthorne and then curving southeasterly into El Segundo. The private right-of-way then curved northeasterly, crossing diagonally through the city. The tracks entered Grand Avenue at Eucalyptus Drive (where the depot was situated) and continued on Grand to Concord Street.

MILEAGES:

South Los Angeles	9.88
Delta (Vermont Avenue)	10.76
Cypave	12.88
Hawthorne	14.42
El Segundo	18.87

FREQUENCY OF SERVICE — 1916: 7 round trips daily.
RUNNING TIME — not available.

Other Southern District Lines

The following lines did not use the "main" Southern District artery from Los Angeles or otherwise reach Los Angeles. Instead, these lines connected other cities with the Southern District.

LONG BEACH-SAN PEDRO LINE

Passenger service on this line began June 25, 1910, and ended January 2, 1949. *Route:* the line went from the Pacific Electric station on Ocean Boulevard and Pacific Avenue in Long Beach on Pacific to Broadway, on Broadway to Pine Avenue, on Pine to Third Street, and on Third to the Los Angeles River, where a private right-of-way on the east side of the river carried tracks to a private bridge adjacent to the Seventh Street bridge. After 1940, the route was west on Ocean Boulevard from Pacific Avenue and over the river. The private right-of-way went up the west bank of the river to approximately Eighth Street and turned northwesterly, crossing Anaheim Street just west of Hayes Avenue. The private right-of-way divided "I" Street from Nicholson Avenue to Mahar Avenue in Wilmington and then continued for five blocks, where it joined the line from Los Angeles (see *San Pedro via Dominguez Line*) and contined to San Pedro.

MILEAGES:

Long Beach	0.00
East Wilmington	4.05
Wilmington (Canal Street)	5.23
San Pedro	7.85

FREQUENCY OF SERVICE — 1911: every 60 minutes (18 round trips daily); 1922: every 40 minutes; 1928: every 30 minutes; 1940: 35 round trips daily; 1941: every 30 minutes; 1944: every 20 minutes; 1948: every 40 minutes.
RUNNING TIME — 1911: 19 minutes to Wilmington and 27 minutes to San Pedro; 1926: 28 minutes to San Pedro; 1932: 23 minutes to San Pedro; 1942: 31 minutes to San Pedro; 1943: 33 minutes to San Pedro; 1948: 30 minutes westbound (to San Pedro) and 31 minutes eastbound (to Long Beach).

SANTA ANA-HUNTINGTON BEACH-BALBOA LINE

Passenger service began in 1907 from Santa Ana to Balboa via Huntington Beach and ended in mid-1912 to points beyond Huntington Beach and to all points in 1922. *Route:* tracks went south from the Pacific Electric station at 421 East Fourth Street in Santa Ana over a private right-of-way to First Street, south in Maple Street to Myrtle Street, and then in a private right-of-way adjacent to Maple Street to Central Avenue. The private right-of-way then curved southeasterly and paralleled Talbert Avenue from Bristol Street to Talbert (later renamed Fountain Valley), continuing south and then easterly. The Pacific Electric station was situated on Lake Avenue at Chicago Street in Huntington Beach. The private right-of-way continued from there to the Los Angeles-Balboa tracks of the Pacific Electric. The line used these tracks to reach Balboa.

MILEAGES:

Santa Ana	0.00
New Delhi	2.69
Acelga	5.60
Talbert (Fountain Valley)	8.16
Bushard	10.53
Huntington Beach	13.31
Newport Beach	18.67
Balboa	20.85

FREQUENCY OF SERVICE — 1911: eight round trips daily plus one round trip between Santa Ana and Huntington Beach only; 1914: 10 round trips daily; 1916: six round trips daily; 1918: one round trip daily; 1921: two round trips daily.
RUNNING TIME 1911: 38 minutes from Santa Ana to Huntington Beach and 51 minutes from Santa Ana to Balboa.

HUNTINGTON BEACH-LA BOLSA LINE

Using a portion of Southern Pacific trackage that was electrified, passenger service started in February, 1911, and ended November 9, 1928. *Route:* from the Pacific Electric station at Chicago Street in Huntington Beach, a private right-of-way paralleled Lake Avenue to Seventeenth Street and then continued northward to the line's terminus at sugar beet processing plants.

MILEAGES:

Huntington Beach	0.00
La Bolsa	1.7
Wiebling	2.84

FREQUENCY OF SERVICE — 1911: 7 outbound and 6 inbound trips daily.
RUNNING TIME — not available for this line.

SANTA ANA-ORANGE LINE

Passenger service on this line began in 1886 and 1887 when it was constructed by the Santa Ana, Orange, and Tustin Street Railway as a horse car line. Henry E. Huntington's Los Angeles Inter-Urban Railroad acquired the line and electrified it in 1906. Passenger service ended on September 14, 1930. *Route:* from the Southern Pacific depot on Fourth Street in Santa Ana, the tracks were on Fourth to Main Street, on Main to a private right-of-way starting approximately across the street from Bullocks' Department Store in Fashion Square, and on the right-of-way to Lemon Street at La Veta Avenue in Orange. The tracks went in a private right-of-way paralleling Lemon to Chapman Avenue, where the line ended.

MILEAGES:

Santa Ana	0.00
Hargraves	2.92
Orange	4.04

FREQUENCY OF SERVICE — 1911: 14 round trips daily; 1916: every 15 minutes from 5:15 a.m. to 6:06 p.m. and every 40 minutes until 11 p.m.; 1921: every 20 minutes during daylight hours and every approximately 45 minutes in the evening.
RUNNING TIME — not available.

A technician services a Big Red Car at the maintenance yards at Long Beach in the late 1950's. Cars were "cannibalized" to keep others rolling when parts were impossible to obtain. (Photo by Maxine Reams)

LONG BEACH-SEAL BEACH LINE

Passenger service from downtown Long Beach to the Alamitos Bay area started in 1904 and was extended to Seal Beach in 1913. Passenger service ended February 24, 1940. *Route:* from Pacific Avenue near Ocean Boulevard the tracks went in Pacific to Broadway, on Broadway to Pine Avenue, north on Pine to Third Street, east on Third to Alamitos Avenue, turning on Alamitos to Broadway, on Broadway to approximately Orizaba Avenue, and then southeasterly over a private right-of-way going diagonally to Grand Avenue and Ocean Boulevard, and then on a private right-of-way dividing Ocean to the San Gabriel River, and over the river on a private bridge to Ocean Avenue in Seal Beach. The tracks went on Ocean to the line's terminus at Ocean and Main Street in Seal Beach.

FREQUENCY OF SERVICE — 1911: every 20 minutes from 6:05 a.m. to 7:25 a.m., and then every 30 minutes until midnight; 1932: every half hour.
RUNNING TIME: 1930: 22 minutes.

NORTHERN DISTRICT

The Pacific Electric's Northern District covered the lines operating in the Pasadena area and stretching eastward as far as Ontario. From downtown Los Angeles, cars travelled a common route to Echandia Junction. Interurbans then rolled directly to their destinations or went through one or as many as five more junctions to reach the ends of the lines. Besides Echandia, the junctions were Valley (originally called Covina Junction), Sierra Vista, Oneonta Park, El Molino, and San Marino.

ECHANDIA JUNCTION: BASIC LOS ANGELES "EXIT" ROUTE

The common route from the Pacific Electric Building at Sixth and Main Streets in downtown Los Angeles was via tracks in Main Street to First Street, in First to Los Angeles Street, in Los Angeles to Aliso Street, and in Aliso (including a bridge over the Los Angeles River) to a private right-of-way paralleling Ramona Boulevard. This right-of-way went north to Echandia Junction (at approximately Mission Road and Marengo Street). After opening of the elevated tracks from the P. E. Building to San Pedro Street, tracks went up San Pedro to Aliso Street. Some routes then went on San Pedro exclusively, while others utilized only Main Street and some used a combination of the two streets for entry and exit.

MILEAGES:

Pacific Electric Station 6th and Main, L.A.)	0.00
1st and Main	.63
Aliso and San Pedro Sts.	1.04
Echandia Junction	2.38

SOUTH PASADENA LINE

Passenger service began May 1, 1895 (as the area's first electric interurban route, built by the Pasadena and Los Angeles Railway Company) and ended January 2, 1935. *Route:* from Echandia Junction, the tracks went on Daly Street to Pasadena Avenue, on Pasadena to a private right-of-way, on this private right-of-way to Roble Avenue, on Roble to a private right-of-way to Mission Street, on Mission to Fair Oaks Avenue, and up Fair Oaks to Colorado Street.

MILEAGES:

Echandia Junction	2.38
Roble Avenue and Avenue 64	7.32
Mission and Fair Oaks	9.24

FREQUENCY OF SERVICE — 1911: every 10 to 20 minutes (approximately 130 round trips daily).

RUNNING TIME — not available.

Valley (formerly "Covina") Junction

From Echandia Junction, a private right-of-way paralleled Ramona Boulevard to Valley Junction (at approximately Ramona Boulevard and Marengo Street). Cars bound for Covina, Pomona, or the San Bernardino and Riverside areas continued eastward through Valley Junction. Trolleys headed for Pasadena or other San Gabriel Valley points went northeasterly through Sierra Vista Junction.

MILEAGES:

Echandia Junction	2.38
Valley (Covina) Junction	3.13

Sierra Vista Junction

From Echandia Junction, a private right-of-way paralleled Ramona Boulevard through Valley Junction (at approximately Ramona and Marengo Street) and then paralleled Soto Street to Huntington Drive. The tracks followed a private right-of-way dividing Huntington Drive to Sierra Vista Junction (at Huntington Drive and Main Street).

MILEAGES:

Echandia Junction	2.38
Valley (Covina) Junction	3.13
Bairdstown	6.16
Sierra Vista	7.42

ALHAMBRA-SAN GABRIEL-TEMPLE CITY LINE

Passenger service to Alhambra and San Gabriel began June 21, 1902, and service on the extension to Temple City started July 29, 1924. Passenger service ended November 29, 1941. *Route:* from Sierra Vista Junction, the tracks were in a private right-of-way dividing Main Street to the Southern Pacific right-of-way (at Raymond Avenue). The tracks then continued eastward in Main, which became Las Tunas Drive in San Gabriel, to the Masonic Home (later the San Gabriel Country Club) between Country Club Drive and California Street. Tracks of the San Gabriel branch went south from Main Street in Mission Drive, passed San Gabriel Mission, were in Junipero Street from the mission to Broadway, and were in a private right-of-way dividing Junipero to San Marino Avenue. The tracks connected to those on Las Tunas via San Marino Avenue. The tracks went eastward on Las Tunas to San Gabriel Boulevard and then followed a private right-of-way dividing Las Tunas to Rosemead Boulevard. From here, the tracks went on Las Tunas to the Pacific Electric station at the northeast corner of Las Tunas and Kauffman Avenue.

MILEAGES:

Sierra Vista Junction	7.42
Palm Avenue	8.21
S. P. Pasadena Branch	8.38
S. P. Monrovia Branch	8.63
Mission Street Junction	10.42
Masonic Home (San Gabriel Valley Country Club)	12.12
Temple City	14.67

FREQUENCY OF SERVICE — 1911: every 15 to 60 minutes (approximately 35 round trips daily); 1924: 51 outbound and 53 inbound trips daily; 1940: approximately 50 round trips daily.

RUNNING TIME — 1911: 17 minutes to Valley (Covina) Junction, 24 minutes to Sierra Vista Junction, 28 minutes to West Alhambra, 37 minutes to Union Street in Alhambra, 45 minutes to San Gabriel Mission, and 50 minutes to the Masonic Home (San Gabriel Valley Country Club); 1940: 52 minutes outbound and 48 minutes inbound (to and from Union Street).

Oneonta Park Junction

The route was to Sierra Vista Junction and then northward on a private right-of-way dividing Huntington Drive to Oneonta Park Junction (at Fair Oaks Avenue).

MILEAGES:

Sierra Vista Junction	7.42
Oneonta Park Junction	8.31

PASADENA SHORT LINE

Passenger service began in 1902 and ended September 30, 1951. *Route:* from Oneonta Park Junction, the route was north in a private right-of-way dividing Fair Oaks Avenue to Monterey Road and then north on Fair Oaks to California Street, on California to Raymond, on Raymond to the Pacific Electric car barns at Fair Oaks and Mary Avenue. Cars leaving Pasadena went down Fair Oaks from Mary Avenue and followed the inbound line after passing California Avenue.

MILEAGES:

Oneonta Park Junction	8.31
Mission and Fair Oaks	9.26
Raymond Hotel	9.87
Colorado and Fair Oaks	11.20

FREQUENCY OF SERVICE — 1911: every 10 to 30 minutes (approximately 70 round trips daily); 1949: every 15 to 60 minutes (approximately 40 round trips daily).

RUNNING TIME — 1911: Los Angeles to Mission and Fair Oaks Avenue, 30 minutes, and Los Angeles to Colorado and Fair Oaks, 38 minutes; 1951: 47 minutes.

EL MOLINO JUNCTION

The route was to Oneonta Park Junction and then eastward in a private right-of-way dividing Huntington Drive to El Molino Junction (at Oak Knoll Avenue).

MILEAGES:

Oneonta Park Junction	8.31
El Molino Junction	10.04

PASADENA OAK KNOLL LINE

Passenger service began in 1906 and ended September 30, 1951. *Route:* the line from Los Angeles went to El Molino Junction and then continued northward on a private right-of-way paralleling Oak Knoll Avenue. The tracks entered Oak Knoll Avenue at approximately Wentworth Avenue, and went on Oak Knoll to Arden Road. The tracks went on Arden to Lake Avenue, north on Lake to Colorado Street, and west on Colorado to Fair Oaks Avenue.

MILEAGES:

El Molino Junction	10.04
Colorado and Lake	11.96
Colorado and Fair Oaks	13.90

FREQUENCY OF SERVICE — 1911: every 15 to 60 minutes (40 round trips daily); 1946: every 15 to 60 minutes (49 round trips daily).

RUNNING TIME — 1911: 17 minutes to Valley (Covina) Junction, 24 minutes to Sierra Vista Junction, 26 minutes to Oneonta Park Junction, 29 minutes to El Molino Junction, and Colorado and Fair Oaks, 45 minutes; 1949: 59 minutes to Colorado and Fair Oaks.

MOUNT LOWE LINE

The line opened July 4, 1893, became a Pasadena and Los Angeles Railway property in 1896, and was acquired by the Pacific Electric in 1902. Service ended after the mountain section of the railway was destroyed by rains in March, 1938. *Route:* the line followed the Pasadena Oak Knoll route to Fair Oaks Avenue and Colorado Street, and then went north on Fair Oaks to Mariposa Street, Altadena. The tracks went east on Mariposa to Lake Avenue, and north on Lake to a private right-of-way beginning approximately 2,600 feet north of Mariposa. This right-of-way led to Rubio Canyon, at Rubio Canyon Road and Loma Alta Drive. Passengers transferred here to the incline railway, which carried them to Echo Mountain. There they boarded narrow gauge trolleys that wound on a right-of-way on the mountains to the Alpine Tavern on Mount Lowe.

MILEAGES:

El Molino Junction	10.04
Pasadena	13.00
Altadena	17.11
Rubio Canyon	18.88
Echo Mountain	19.38
Cape of Good Hope	20.25
Dawn	20.61
Circular Bridge	21.15
Granite Gate	22.00
Alpine Tavern	22.95

FREQUENCY OF SERVICE — 1911: 5 round trips from Los Angeles and 2 round trips from Pasadena.

RUNNING TIME — 1911: 17 minutes to Valley (Covina) Junction, 24 minutes to Sierra Vista Junction, 26 minutes to Oneonta Park Junction, 30 minutes to El Molino Junction, 50 minutes to Pasadena, 65 minutes to Altadena, 75 minutes to Rubio Canyon, 90 minutes to Cape of Good Hope, 95 minutes to Dawn, 100 minutes to Circular Bridge, 106 minutes to Granite Gate, and 120 minutes to Alpine Tavern.

San Marino Junction

From El Molino Junction, the route was on a private right-of-way dividing Huntington Drive to Sierra Madre Boulevard.

MILEAGES:

El Molino Junction	10.04
San Marino Junction	11.35

SIERRA MADRE LINE

Passenger service began March 19, 1904, and ended October 6, 1950. *Route:* the line followed the one from Los Angeles to San Marino Junction and then turned north on a private right-of-way to Sierra Madre Boulevard to Michillinda Avenue. From there, the track continued in Sierra Madre to Kersting Court. The track went on Kersting to Baldwin Avenue (where the station was situated) and then continued over a private right-of-way to its terminus at Mountain Trail Avenue.

MILEAGES:

San Marino Junction	11.35
El Camino	13.15
El Rincon	14.27
Sierra Madre	16.70
Wilson Trail	17.03

FREQUENCY OF SERVICE — 1911: every 20 to 60 minutes (18 round trips daily); 1946: 19 round trips daily; 1948: 11 trains outbound and 9 trains inbound daily.

RUNNING TIME — 1911: 17 minutes to Valley (Covina) Junction, 26 minutes to Sierra Vista Junction, 32 minutes to El Molino Junction, 34 minutes to San Marino, and 52 minutes to Sierra Madre; 1948: 63 minutes to Sierra Madre.

MONROVIA-GLENDORA LINE

Passenger service began March 1, 1903, to Monrovia and in April, 1907, to Glendora. Passenger service ended September 30, 1951. *Route:* the line followed the one from Los Angeles to San Marino Junction. The tracks then continued eastward in a private right-of-way dividing Huntington Drive through San Marino and Arcadia, where at approximately San Rafael Road the tracks curved northward on a private right-of-way and at Santa Anita Avenue went eastward on Santa Clara Avenue to to Second Avenue. The tracks continued eastward on a private right-of-way that would have been an extension of Santa Clara. The tracks entered Chestnut Avenue at Esplanade Avenue, continuing east on Chestnut past the Pacific Electric station (at the northeast corner of Chestnut and Myrtle Avenue) to Canyon Boulevard. The tracks continued eastward on a private right-of-way following what would have been an extension of Chestnut to approximately Mountain Avenue, where the tracks curved northward to a private right-of-way paralleling Royal Oaks Drive. At Fish Canyon Road (Las Lomas Avenue), the private right-of-way turned southeasterly, and after entering Azusa paralleled Crescent Drive from Vernon Avenue to Orange Avenue, where the tracks entered Ninth Street. The Pacific Electric station was south of Ninth between Angeleno and Azusa Avenues. The route was on Ninth to approximately Pasadena Avenue, where a private right-of-way continued eastward, paralleling the Santa Fe right-of-way to approximately Trayer Avenue in Glendora. The tracks entered Glendora on Mountain View Avenue and ended at Pennsylvania Avenue.

MILEAGES:

San Marino Junction	11.35
Sunnyslope	14.46
Arcadia	16.24
Monrovia	18.26
Duarte	19.82
Puente Largo	21.56
Azusa	23.32
Glendora	25.99

FREQUENCY OF SERVICE — 1911: 29 outbound trains daily to Monrovia (11 of which continued to Glendora) and 31 inbound trains daily to Monrovia (12 of which started in Glendora; 1943: 47 round trips daily (25 of which continued to Glendora).

RUNNING TIME — 1911: 31 minutes to San Marino, 42 minutes to Arcadia, 47 minutes to Monrovia, 51 minutes to Duarte, 60 minutes to Azusa, and 68 minutes to Glendora; 1943: 37 minutes to San Marino, 51 minutes to Arcadia, 57 minutes to Monrovia, 78 minutes to Azusa, and 80 minutes to Glendora.

Valley (formerly "Covina") Junction

The route from Echandia Junction was over a private right-of-way paralleling Ramona Boulevard to Valley Junction (at approximately Cornwell Street). Much of the right-of-way was covered by the San Bernardino Freeway.

MILEAGES:

Valley (Covina) Junction	3.13

COVINA-POMONA LINE

Passenger service to Covina began in 1907 and to Pomona on August 31, 1912. *Route:* the line was over a private right-of-way paralleling Ramona Boulevard from Valley Junction to approximately Rockwell Avenue in El Monte. Portions of the San Bernardino Freeway have covered many parts of the right-of-way. From Rockwell, a private right-of-way went eastward, paralleling San Bernardino Road (which became Ramona Boulevard in Baldwin Park) from Valley Boulevard to approximately Harlan Avenue. From Harlan, a private right-of-way divided Ramona Boulevard to Downing Avenue. The private right-of-way then cut northeasterly, paralleling Los Angeles Avenue from approximately Elton Avenue to Azusa Canyon Road. The tracks then continued eastward on a private right-of-way to Grand Avenue in Covina. The right-of-way then cut northeasterly and at Valley Center Avenue headed eastward. In La Verne, the right-of-way turned southwesterly, paralleling Orange Street to the P. E. station between "D" and "E" streets. From here, the tracks curved southward on a private right-of-way between White Avenue and Huntington Boulevard, passing the Los Angeles County Fairgrounds and Ganesha Park. The tracks went down White Avenue to Holt Avenue, on Holt to Garey Avenue, south on Garey to Franklin Avenue, and east on Franklin to the route's terminus at Palomares Avenue.

MILEAGES:

Valley (Covina) Junction	3.13
Granada Park	6.40
Ramona	8.15
Wilmar	9.51
El Monte	13.14
Baldwin Park	18.00
Covina	21.79
San Dimas (P. E. Station)	26.29
San Dimas (S. P. Station)	26.35
Lordsburg (La Verne)	28.53
Pomona Junction	30.89
Pomona	31.89

FREQUENCY OF SERVICE — 1911: 21 round trips daily, of which 1 went only to and from El Monte and seven went to and six from San Dimas; 1912: 12 round trips daily to Pomona; 1920: 19 round trips daily to Pomona and 31 round trips daily to Covina; 1940: 18 round trips daily to Pomona; 1946: 5 round trips daily to Covina and 43 round trips daily to Baldwin Park.

RUNNING TIME — 1911: 23 minutes to Granada Park, 31 minutes to Wilmar, 39 minutes to El Monte, 49 minutes to Baldwin Park, 60 minutes to Covina, and 72 minutes to San Dimas; 1916: 22 minutes to Granada Park, 30 minutes to Wilmar, 39 minutes to El Monte, 60 minutes to Covina, 65 minutes to San Dimas, and 83 minutes to Pomona; 1920: 84 minutes to Pomona; 1946: 36 minutes to Wilmar, 46 minutes to El Monte, and 61 minutes to Baldwin Park.

Other Northern District Interurban Routes

The following routes also were operated in the Pacific Electric's Northern District, linking cities within the area. They did not, however, connect directly to Los Angeles.

ONTARIO-SAN ANTONIO HEIGHTS LINE

The Ontario and San Antonio Heights Railway Company was established in 1887 and used mules to haul passener cars. (The mules pulled the cars up the line and got a free ride down on a platform.) Acquired by the Ontario Electric Company, the line was electrified in 1895 and became part of the Pacific Light and Power Company when it absorbed Ontario Electric in 1908. Pacific Electric purchased the railway in 1912 and merged it into the P. E. system. Passenger service was discontinued to 24th Street on July 4, 1924, to Upland on November 1, 1924, and on the balance of the line on October 6, 1928. *Route:* the line was from Emporia Street and Euclid Avenue in Ontario up a private right-of-way dividing Euclid to La Cima (24th Street), where the right-of-way turned west and continued to San Antonio Heights.

MILEAGES:

Ontario	0.00
Upland	2.59
San Antonio Heights	7.54

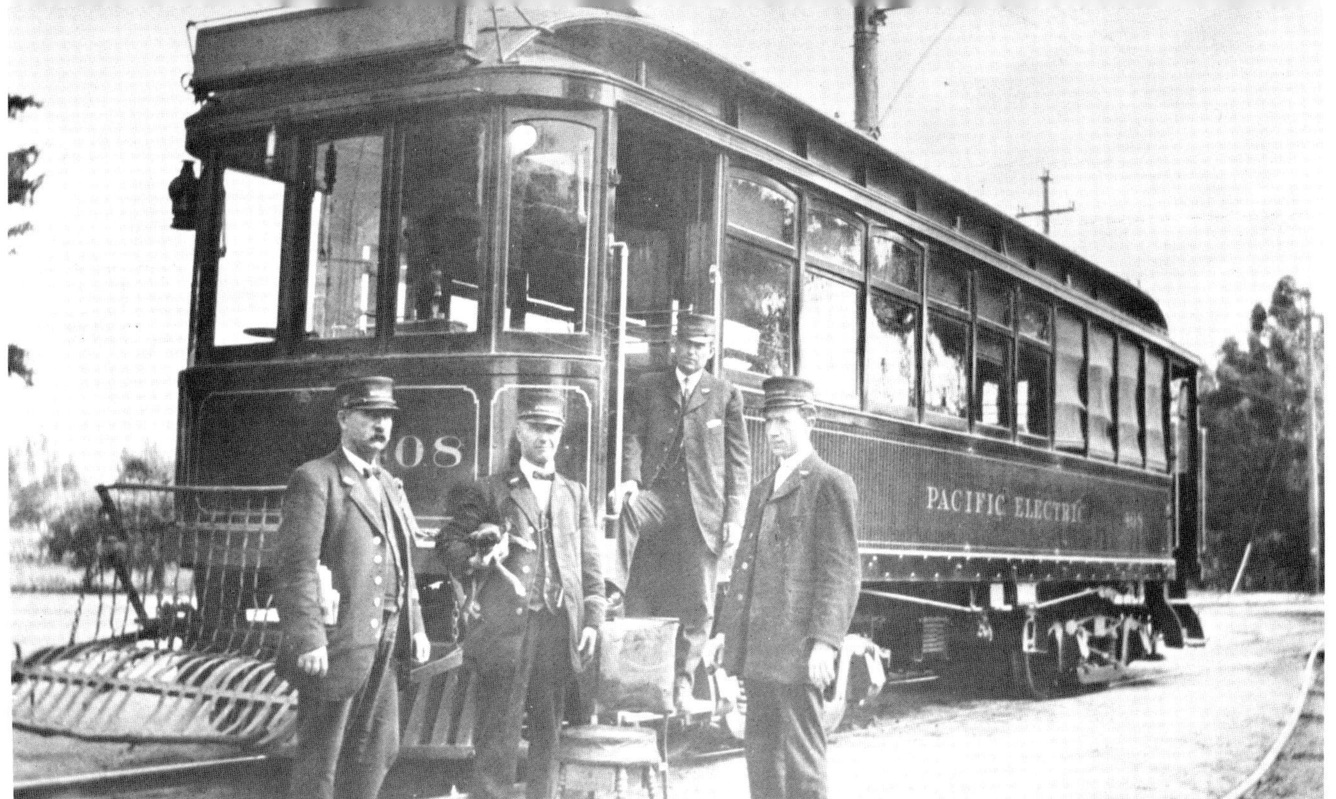

These trolleymen posed for this photograph while serving on the interurban line to Redondo Beach. The time was approximately 1916. (Historical Collections: Security Pacific National Bank)

FREQUENCY OF SERVICE — 1916: 20 round trips daily.

RUNNING TIME — 1916: 9 minutes from Ontario to Upland, and 25 minutes from Upland to San Antonio Heights.

POMONA-UPLAND LINE

The line was built in 1910 by the Ontario and San Antonio Heights Railway Company, which was acquired in 1912 by the Pacific Electric. Passenger service began January 1, 1911, and ended January 1, 1933. *Route:* the line was from the Pacific Electric station at Third Street and Garey Avenue in Pomona north on Garey to Walnut Street, where tracks went in a private right-of-way to the P. E. main line between Los Angeles and San Bernardino. The route followed this line to Euclid Avenue in Upland.

MILEAGES:

Pomona (Salt Lake R.R. Station)	0.00
Claremont	.50
West Upland	6.87
West Ontario	8.07
Upland	11.69
Ontario	10.50
San Antonio Heights	13.07

FREQUENCY OF SERVICE — 1916: 33 round trips daily (of which 10 ended at North Pomona).

RUNNING TIME — 1916: 12 minutes to North Pomona, 17 minutes to Claremont, 27 minutes to Upland, and 39 minutes to Ontario.

EASTERN DISTRICT

The lines the farthest from Los Angeles operated in the Pacific Electric's Eastern District, which covered trolley lines in San Bernardino County east of Ontario and those in Riverside County. The electric cars followed the line to Pomona as far as Lordsburg (LaVerne).

SAN BERNARDINO LINE

Passenger service to San Bernardino began June 11, 1914, and ended November 1, 1941. *Route:* the line from Los Angeles followed the one to Pomona to the P. E. station on Orange Street between "D" and "B" streets in LaVerne. From here, a private right-of-way curved northeasterly and then headed east, paralleling the Santa Fe Railroad right-of-way through Claremont to approximately Berkeley Avenue, where the tracks paralleled First Street to approximately Mills Avenue. There the tracks entered a private right-of-way dividing Huntington Drive to Benson Avenue, where the private right-of-way continued midway between Arrow Highway and Ninth Street. The tracks entered San Bernardino on Third Street and the P. E. station was on the south side of Third between "E" and "F" streets.

MILEAGES:

Lordsburg	28.75
North Pomona	30.32
Claremont	31.82
Upland	35.91
Alta Loma	39.39
Etiwanda	43.71
Fontana	49.17
Rialto	52.92
San Bernardino	57.41

FREQUENCY OF SERVICE — 1916: 7 round trips daily; 1934: 8 round trips daily; 1937: 9 round trips daily; 1940: 4 round trips daily.

RUNNING TIME — 1916: 125 minutes; 1931: 110 minutes; 1935: 119 minutes; 1940: 105 minutes.

SAN BERNARDINO-RIVERSIDE LINE

Passenger service began October 14, 1913, and ended May 8, 1939. *Route:* the line from the Pacific Electric station on the south side of Third Street between "E" and "F" Streets went south on a private right-of-way midway between "E" and "F" to Mill Street, and continued south in a private right-of-way dividing Mount Vernon Avenue to "I" Street in Colton. From here, the tracks went down Ninth Street to "O" Street and then south over a private right-of-way to approximately West Highgrove Street in Riverside, where the right-of-way paralleled La Cadena Drive (formerly Colton Avenue) to First Street; the line went west on First to Main Street, and south on Main to 14th Street.

MILEAGES:

Riverside (14th and Main)	0.00
Vine	1.42
Market Junction	1.62
Palmyrita	3.11
Grand Terrace	5.44
Revino	5.87
Congress	6.99
Colton (S. P. Crossing)	7.63
Mount Vernon	8.43
Shop Siding	10.63
San Bernardino	10.94

FREQUENCY OF SERVICE — 1935: every 37 to 60 minutes (13 round trips daily).

RUNNING TIME — 1935: 9 minutes

to Colton and 34 minutes to Riverside (14th and Main Streets).

REDLANDS LINE

Passenger service between Redlands and San Bernardino began March 3, 1903, and between Redlands and Los Angeles on June 11, 1914. Passenger service ended July 20, 1936. *Route:* from the Pacific Electric station on the south side of Third Street between "E" and "F" Streets in San Bernardino, the line was east on Third Street to "A" Street, curving onto a private right-of-way paralleling Mill Street to Mountain View Street, south on a private right-of-way adjacent to Mountain View to San Bernardino Avenue, on a right-of-way adjacent to Mountain View to Orange Avenue, and south on Orange to the terminus at Citrus Avenue.

MILEAGES:	
San Bernardino	0.00
Allen Street	.91
Race Track	2.14
Amen	2.84
Gravel Pit	3.31
Marigold	4.62
Crown Jewel	6.08
Sunkist	7.09
Lugonia	8.16
Casa Loma	8.56
Redlands (P. E. Station)	9.16

FREQUENCY OF SERVICE — 1903: every 40 to 50 minutes (20 round trips daily); 1908: every 30 to 45 minutes (25 round trips daily); 1912: every 40 minutes (29 round trips daily); 1916: every 60 minutes; 1935: 6 outbound and 5 inbound trips daily.

RUNNING TIME — 1903: 40 minutes outbound and 35 minutes inbound; 1908: 32 minutes outbound and 28 minutes inbound; 1935: 26 minutes.

RIVERSIDE-REDLANDS LINE

Passenger service began in 1916 and ended May 8, 1939. *Route:* the line was composed of through-routing of the line from Riverside to San Bernardino and San Bernardino to Redlands.

MILEAGES:	
Riverside (14th and Main)	0.00
Vine	1.42
Market Junction	1.62
Palmyrita	3.11
Grand Terrace	5.44
Revino	5.87
Congress	6.99
Colton (S. P. Crossing)	7.63
Mount Vernon	8.43
Shop Siding	10.63
San Bernardino	10.94
Allen Street	11.85
Race Track	13.08
Amen	13.78
Gravel Pit	14.25
Marigold	15.56
Crown Jewel	17.02
Sunkist	18.03
Lugonia	19.10
Casa Loma	19.50
Redlands (P. E. Station)	20.10

FREQUENCY OF SERVICE — 1927: every 40 to 60 minutes; 1935: 7 round trips daily.

RUNNING TIME — 1935: 50 minutes.

SAN BERNARDINO-COLTON LINE

The line was built by the San Bernardino Valley Traction Company and opened for service February 22, 1902. Passenger service ended February 22, 1942. *Route:* the line from San Bernardino was from "D" Street west on Third Street to Mount Vernon Avenue, south on Mount Vernon to Hubbard Street, and then over a private right-of-way to Eighth Street in Colton. The tracks went south in Eighth Street to "J" Street and east on "J" to Ninth Street.

MILEAGES:	
San Bernardino ("D" and Third)	0.00
P. E. Station	.14
Santa Fe Station	.86
La Cadena	2.87
Colton ("J" and Ninth)	4.24

FREQUENCY OF SERVICE — 1903: every 30 to 60 minutes (approximately 30 round trips daily); 1912: every 20 to 40 minutes (approximately 30 round trips daily); 1924: every 15 to 30 minutes (approximately 75 round trips daily).

RUNNING TIME — 1903: 20 minutes.

ARROWHEAD SPRINGS LINE

Built by the San Bernardino Valley Traction Company, the line opened March 15, 1907. Passenger service ended January 2, 1925. *Route:* the line went from the Pacific Electric station on the south side of Third Street between "E" and "F" Streets east on Third Street to "D" Street, north on "D" to Highland Avenue, east on Highland to Mountain View Avenue, and then north in a private right-of-way dividing Mountain View. From Mountain View, the track followed a private right-of-way to Arrowhead Springs.

MILEAGES:	
San Bernardino (P. E. Station)	0.00
Highland Avenue	2.55
Severance	5.00
Arrowhead Springs	7.25

FREQUENCY OF SERVICE — 1907: 7 round trips daily; 1912: 8 round trips daily; 1914: 6 round trips daily; 1920: 5 round trips daily; 1922: 6 round trips daily.

RUNNING TIME — 1921: 35 minutes outbound and 28 minutes inbound.

HIGHLAND-PATTON LINE

The line was constructed in 1903 by the San Bernardino Traction Company, and passenger service began August 13, 1903. Passenger service to Patton ended June 1, 1924, and to Highland on July 20, 1936. *Route:* the line went from the Pacific Electric station on the south side of Third Street between "E" and "F" Streets east on Third Street to "D" Street, north on "D" to Seventh Street, east on Seventh to "A" Street and then southeasterly over a private right-of-way to Waterman Avenue and Sixth Street. The right-of-way then went easterly over a private right-of-way representing an extension of Sixth to Pepper Avenue; the line went north on Pepper to Second Street (Harlem Springs), east on Second to Central Avenue, north on Central to Pacific Avenue, and east on Pacific to Palm Avenue in Highland. The Patton Line went north from Patton Junction (Central and Pacific Avenues) on Central to Patton.

MILEAGES: (To Highland)	
San Bernardino (P. E. Station)	0.00
"C" Street	.20
Cemetery	.90
Antill	2.02
Sterling	3.33
Harlem	5.25
Patton Junction	6.05
Highland	6.56

MILEAGES: (To Patton)	
Patton Junction	6.05
Patton	6.57

FREQUENCY OF SERVICE — 1912: every 60 minutes (18 round trips daily, of which half made the side trips to Patton when inbound); 1921: 11 round trips daily (4 of the trips when to Patton); 1924: 6 round trips daily; 1932: 3 round trips daily.

RUNNING TIME — 1924: 22 minutes outbound and 25 minutes inbound.

LOS ANGELES-RIVERSIDE LINE

Passenger service between Riverside and the Riverside Portland Cement Company at Crestmore began in 1908, to Bloomington on May 20, 1911, and to Rialto on March 24, 1914. Passenger service between Los Angeles and Riverside started March 15, 1915, and service was discontinued June 9, 1940. *Route:* the line from Los Angeles followed the one from Los Angeles to San Bernardino to Rialto Junction, and then turned south on a private right-of-way dividing Riverside Avenue in Rialto. The private right-of-way then turned southwesterly to Bloomington, and then headed southeasterly through Crestmore. Cars left the right-of-way and entered Riverside on Market Street, going south on Market past the Pacific Electric station on the east side of Market between Seventh and Eighth Streets to 14th Street.

MILEAGES:	
Rialto	52.92
Poole	53.92
Bloomington	56.42
Cement Plant	58.82
Alvarado	60.91
Alamo	61.37
Hancock	61.81
Riverside (P. E. Station)	62.50
Riverside (14th and Market)	63.08

FREQUENCY OF SERVICE — 1916: five outbound and six inbound trips between Los Angeles and Riverside daily; 1938: one round trip daily.

RUNNING TIME: 1916: 137 minutes.

RIVERSIDE-RIALTO LINE

Passenger service began May 20, 1911, to Bloomington and March 24, 1914, to Rialto. Passenger service ended June 9, 1940. *Route:* the line followed the Los

ABOVE: A Highland-bound interurban waited in the San Bernardino P. E. station about 1915. BELOW: This trolley with open ends served San Pedro and was operated by Los Angeles Inter-Urban, used by Henry Huntington to fight the S. P. (Both Photos: Stephen D. Maguire Collection)*

A conductor closes a safety gate as the motorman prepares to start this trolley operating in the early 1900's between Edendale, near Glendale, and Los Angeles. (Stephen D. Maguire Collection)

Angeles-Riverside route between Rialto and Riverside.

MILEAGES: (*See Los Angeles-Riverside Line*)

FREQUENCY OF SERVICE — 1914: approximately 10 round trips daily; 1931: 9 round trips daily; 1939: 4 round trips daily; 1940: 1 round trip daily.

RUNNING TIME — 1914: 28 minutes to Bloomington and 38 minutes to Rialto.

RIVERSIDE-CORONA LINE

Passenger service began on February 17, 1915. Passenger service between Arlinton and Corona ended August 31, 1931, and from Riverside to Arlington on January 10, 1943. *Route:* from Sixth and Main Streets in Riverside, the line was south on Main to 14th Street, and then south on Magnolia Avenue to Arlington; the tracks then followed a private right-of-way dividing Magnolia Avenue to Corona, where the line went in Third Street to Merrill Avenue.

MILEAGES:

Riverside (6th and Main)	0.00
Central Avenue	2.25
Arlington	6.62
May Tower	12.60
Corona (3rd and Merrill)	14.53

FREQUENCY OF SERVICE — 1913: every 20 minutes to Arlington; 1927: every two hours to Corona; 1943: every 30 minutes to Arlington.

RUNNING TIME — 38 minutes outbound and 43 minutes inbound between Riverside and Arlington; 1924: 20 minutes outbound and 23 minutes inbound; 1927: 37 minutes between Riverside and Corona.

WESTERN DISTRICT

The Pacific Electric's Western District was formed through the consolidation of the Los Angeles Pacific Railroad routes, which served Hollywood, Beverly Hills, Santa Monica, Venice, and adjacent areas, and the Los Angeles and Redondo Railway. The Glendale Line, part of Henry Huntington's original Pacific Electric, also was included in the district since the route was westerly from downtown Los Angeles. The lines to the San Fernando Valley and Burbank, constructed after the formation in 1911 of the consolidated Pacific Electric, also operated within the Western District.

Many Western District lines operated from the Hollywood Subway after its opening in 1925. The subway began beneath the Subway Terminal Building at 417 South Hill Street in downtown Los Angeles and extended 4,325 feet, emerging southeast of Beverly Boulevard and Glendale Boulevard. Cars entered Glendale Boulevard, going on Glendale to Sunset Boulevard where they resumed their previous routes.

SANTA MONICA VIA SAWTELLE LINE

Passenger service from Los Angeles to Santa Monica began in 1897 and to Venice in 1901. Service ended July 7, 1940. *Route:* the line followed the Venice Short Line to Vineyard Junction. From here, the tracks were in a private right-of-way in the center of San Vicente Boulevard to Burton Way and in a private right-of-way adjacent to Burton Way from there to Santa Monica Boulevard; the line continued in a private right-of-way dividing Santa Monica Boulevard to Sepulveda Boulevard. The tracks then went in Santa Monica Boulevard to Ocean Avenue, and in Ocean Avenue and Trolleyway to Windward Avenue.

MILEAGES:

Vineyard Junction	5.56
Carthay Center	7.73
Beverly Hills	10.18
Sawtelle	13.36
Santa Monica	17.12
Ocean Park (Pier Avenue)	18.49
Venice (Windward Avenue)	19.33

FREQUENCY OF SERVICE — 1911: every 30 minutes (38 round trips daily); 1934: every 40 minutes.

RUNNING TIME — 1911: 23 minutes to Vineyard, 32 minutes to Beverly Hills, 38 minutes to Sawtelle, 52 minutes to Santa Monica, 60 minutes to Ocean Park, and 64 minutes to Venice; 1934: 60 minutes to Santa Monica.

HOLLYWOOD-VENICE LINE

Passenger service began in the late 1890's and ended on August 23, 1941. *Route:* from Fourth and Hill Streets in downtown Los Angeles, the tracks went north on Hill to Sunset Boulevard, west on Sunset to Hollywood Boulevard, west on Hollywood to La Brea Avenue and south through Crescent Junction (originally Gardner Junction) over a private right-of-way emerging through Crescent Heights Boulevard onto Santa Monica Boulevard, and then over a private right-of-way dividing Santa Monica Boulevard on the line used by the Beverly Hills via Sawtelle Line to Venice.

MILEAGES:

Los Angeles (4th and Hill)	0.00
Bonnie Brae Street	2.65
Gardner (Crescent) Junction (La Brea Avenue)	8.70
Beverly Hills	12.19

Sawtelle	15.37
Santa Monica	19.13
Ocean Park (Pier Avenue)	20.50
Venice (Windward Avenue)	21.34

FREQUENCY OF SERVICE — 1911: every 30 minutes (approximately 40 round trips daily); 1920: approximately 20 trips daily

RUNNING TIME — 1911: Los Angeles to: Hollywood, 31 minutes, Beverly Hills, 48 minutes, Sawtelle, 54 minutes, Santa Monica, 68 minutes, and Venice, 80 minutes; 1927: Los Angeles to Venice, 93 minutes.

MILEAGES:

Los Angeles	0.00
Vineyard	5.56
Culver City	9.25
Palms	10.05
Ocean Park Heights	11.95
Venice (Windward Avenue)	14.81
Ocean Park (Pier Avenue)	15.65
Santa Monica (Santa Monica Blvd. and Broadway)	17.02

FREQUENCY OF SERVICE — 1911: every 15 to 30 minutes (53 round trips daily); 1948: every 7 to 20 minutes (55 round trips daily).

RUNNING TIME — 1911: 22 min- (approximately 40 round trips daily.)

RUNNING TIME — 1927: Los Angeles to: Beverly Hills, 40 minutes, Sawtelle, 48 minutes, and Santa Monica, 75 minutes.

INGLEWOOD LINE

Passenger service began in 1902 over trackage built in 1887 by the Santa Fe Railroad and leased for electrification to the Los Angeles and Pacific. Passenger service ended in 1928. *Route:* from Ocean Park, the line went on a private right-of-way paralleling Neilson Way to Loma Avenue in Venice, and then paralleling Washington Boulevard to Washington

Trolleymen pose by an interurban at Vineyard Junction in West Los Angeles in approximately 1916. The car was operating to the Laurel Canyon area of Hollywood. (Craig Rasmussen Collection)

VENICE SHORT LINE

Passenger service began in 1903 and was discontinued September 17, 1950. *Route:* from the Hill Street station at Fourth and Hill Streets in downtown Los Angeles, the line originally went south on Hill Street to Venice Boulevard, on Venice to Pacific Avenue, over a private right-of-way to Normandie Avenue, on Venice Boulevard to Arlington Avenue, over a private right-of-way and Blaine Street to Concord Street, and then along a private right-of-way to Vineyard Junction (between Pico and Venice Boulevards and Highland Avenue and West Boulevard). The line then went on a private right-of-way paralleling Venice Boulevard to Pacific Avenue in Venice, on Pacific to Windward Avenue, on a private right-of-way paralleling Pacific Avenue to Ocean Avenue and on Ocean to Pico Boulevard. From there, the tracks went over a private right-of-way to the Pacific Electric station at Third Street and Santa Monica Boulevard.

utes to Vineyard, 30 minutes to Palms, 38 minutes to Venice, 42 minutes to Ocean Park, and 50 minutes to Santa Monica; 1941: 64 minutes to Venice.

WESTGATE LINE

Passenger service began in 1906 and ended June 30, 1940. *Route:* the line followed the Santa Monica via Beverly Hills line to Sawtelle, where it turned north at Purdue Avenue onto a private right-of-way. From Wilshire Boulevard, this track was on a right-of-way dividing San Vicente Boulevard to Ocean Avenue in Santa Monica. The line then went on Ocean Avenue to its terminus at Santa Monica Boulevard.

MILEAGES:

Sawtelle	13.36
Santa Monica	19.42

FREQUENCY OF SERVICE — 1911: every 60 minutes between 7:25 a.m. and 6:25 p.m.; 1913: 2 round trips daily; 1927: every 30 minutes during rush hours

Way; from here, the right-of-way went east, paralleling Jefferson Boulevard from a point just west of Grosvenor Boulevard to Centinela Avenue, curving on a parallel with Florence Avenue to Centinela Avenue and following Centinela to approximately the 5900 block. The right-of-way paralleled Thornburn Street from Alvern Street to Venice Way, Hyde Park Boulevard from Venice Way to Glenway Drive, and Ballona Boulevard to the Pacific Electric station on Eucalyptus Avenue.

MILEAGES:

Ocean Park	0.00
Milwood Junction	.64
Machado	2.04
Alla	2.66
Inglewood	7.23

FREQUENCY OF SERVICE — 1911: one round trip daily.

RUNNING TIME — not available.

Youngsters enjoyed riding the P. E. system, once an important part of Southern California life. The author (in white tie) and his mother, Mrs. Jessie Person Crump (in white blouse to the left), had their photograph taken with other passengers during a Mount Lowe excursions during the 1930's.

SANTA MONICA AIR LINE

Passenger service began in 1908 on this line, developed on the right-of-way of the Los Angeles and Independence Railroad opened in 1875 between Santa Monica and Los Angeles and acquired in 1877 by the Southern Pacific. The S. P. leased the line to the Los Angeles and Pacific, which electrified it. Passenger service was discontinued on October 26, 1953. *Route:* from the Pacific Electric Building at Sixth and Main Streets in downtown Los Angeles, cars followed the Long Beach line to Amoco Junction (at 25th Street) and then went southwesterly over a private right-of-way; at Figueroa Street, this right-of-way divided Exposition Boulevard to 34th Street in Santa Monica. The right-of-way continued, paralleling Colorado Avenue from 20th Street to Lincoln Boulevard; the tracks went on Lincoln to Ocean Avenue, and on Ocean to Ocean Park.

MILEAGES:	
Los Angeles	0.00
Amoco Junction	2.62
San Pedro Street	3.76
Grand Avenue	4.54
U.S.C.	5.40
Culver Junction	11.16
Palms	12.19
Santa Monica	16.85
Ocean Park	19.20

FREQUENCY OF SERVICE — 1911: 1 round trip daily; 1913: every 60 minutes; 1920: every 30 to 90 minutes to Culver Junction and 1 round trip daily to Santa Monica;

RUNNING TIME — 1911: 40 minutes.

REDONDO BEACH-DEL REY LINE

Passenger service to Playa del Rey began in 1902 and to Redondo Beach in 1903. Passenger service ended May 12, 1940. *Route:* from Los Angeles, the line followed the Venice Short Line to Culver City. The tracks then were in a private right-of-way dividing Culver Boulevard to Lincoln Boulevard, and from there followed a private right-of-way to Vista del Mar Boulevard in Playa del Rey. The tracks went in Vista del Mar to the ocean front and then went in a private right-of-way paralleling the coast to Homer Avenue in Hermosa Beach. The private right-of-way continued, paralleling Shakespeare Avenue to Hawthorne Avenue; from here, the right-of-way divided Hermosa Avenue to Redondo Beach. The tracks went in Hermosa Avenue to a junction with the Santa Fe Railroad line at Pacific Avenue, and then went on Pacific to Catalina Avenue, and on Catalina to Clifton.

MILEAGES:	
Culver Junction	9.25
Playa del Rey	15.10
Manhattan Beach	20.59
Hermosa Beach	22.29
Redondo Beach	24.06
Clifton	25.07

FREQUENCY OF SERVICE — 1911: 30 round trips daily; 1931: 24 outbound and 22 inbound trips.

RUNNING TIME — 1911: Los Angeles to Vineyard Junction, 23 minutes; Los Angeles to Playa del Rey, 43 minutes, Los Angeles to Manhattan Beach, 53 minutes, and Los Angeles to Redondo Beach, 63 minutes; 1940: 87 minutes.

SAN FERNANDO VALLEY LINE

Passenger service started to Van Nuys on December 16, 1911, to Owensmouth (Canoga Park) on December 7, 1912, and to San Fernando on March 22, 1913. Service to Owensmouth and San Fernando was discontinued June 1, 1938 and service to Van Nuys ended December 28, 1952. *Route:* the line originally went from Fourth and Hill Streets in downtown Los Angeles north to Sunset Boulevard. When the Subway Terminal opened in 1925, the route was from there via the subway to Glendale Boulevard, on Glendale to Park Avenue, on Park to Sunset Boulevard, on Sunset to Santa Monica Boulevard, on Santa Monica to Highland Avenue, and on Highland to Cahuenga Pass. A private right-of-way paralleled the highway through the pass and along Cahuenga Boulevard to Vineland Avenue. The route was up Vineland to Weddington Street, where the tracks turned onto a private right-of-way dividing Chandler Boulevard. The line followed Chandler to Van Nuys Boulevard. The route was then on a private right-of-way in Van Nuys to the Southern Pacific tracks near Aetna Street, where the tracks continued in Van Nuys Boulevard. The private right-of-way in Van Nuys Boulevard resumed at Van Owen Street and continued to Sherman Circle, where the tracks curved into a private right-of-way in Sherman Way. They continued in Sherman Way to Etiwanda Avenue, where they were laid in Sherman Way to Vanalden Avenue. There they resumed the private right-of-way dividing Sherman Way, continuing to Variel Avenue. The tracks were laid in Sherman Way to Topanga Canyon Boulevard, terminus of the line.

MILEAGES: (To North Sherman Way Junction)	
Los Angeles	0.00
Highland and Santa Monica	7.09
Highland and Hollywood Boulevard	7.84
Cahuenga Pass	8.56
Hollywood Way	9.99
Universal City	11.10
Rio Vista	11.59
North Hollywood	14.17
Kester Junction	16.17
Circle Drive	17.72
Van Nuys	19.11
North Sherman Way	19.89

MILEAGES: (To San Fernando)	
North Sherman Way Junction	19.89
Mission Acres	22.81
Plummer	23.81
San Fernando	27.47

MILEAGES: (To Owensmouth)	
North Sherman Way Junction	19.89
Reseda	24.91
Owensmouth (Canoga Park)	29.10

FREQUENCY OF SERVICE — 1912: 10 round trips daily to Van Nuys; 1913: 7 round trips daily to Owensmouth (Canoga Park); 1913: 6 round trips daily to San Fernando (City); 1918: 10 round trips daily to San Fernando (City); 1929: 27 cars daily left Los Angeles for the San Fernando Valley and after alternate switching or division of two-car trains, 17 cars went to Owensmouth (Canoga Park) and 16 went to San Fernando (City); 1944: every 20 minutes.

RUNNING TIME — 1912: to Van Nuys, 70 minutes outbound and 65 minutes inbound; 1913: to Owensmouth (Canoga Park), 95 minutes; 1913: to San Fernando (City), 80 minutes outbound and 78 minutes inbound; 1931: to San Fernando (City), 78 minutes; 1952: to Van Nuys, 89 minutes outbound and 87 minutes inbound.

GLENDALE-BURBANK LINE

Passenger service to Glendale began April 6, 1904, and to Burbank on September 6, 1911. Passenger service ended June 19, 1955. *Route:* the line originally went from the Southern Pacific's Arcade Station at Fifth, Central, and Ceres Streets in downtown Los Angeles on Ceres to Sixth Street, on Sixth to Olive Avenue, on Olive to Seventh Street, on Seventh to Figueroa Street, on Figueroa to Second Street, and on Second to Glendale Boulevard. After opening of the Subway Terminal in 1925, cars left through the Subway to Glendale Boulevard, and at Sunset Boulevard entered a private right-of-way dividing Glendale Boulevard. This right-of-way continued to Effie Street, where tracks returned to Glendale Boulevard. At Alessandro Street, the tracks entered a private right-of-way through the Ivanhoe Hills and spanning the Los Angeles River by a bridge. The tracks then resumed a private right-of-way dividing Glendale Boulevard; at San Fernando Road (city limits of Glendale), Glendale Boulevard became Brand Boulevard, with the tracks continuing in Brand to Mountain Street. Burbank Branch: at Arden Junction, the line turned from Brand and went west in a private right-of-way dividing Glenoaks to Eton Drive.

MILEAGES: (Glendale)	
Los Angeles	0.00
Ivanhoe	5.71
San Fernando Road	6.85
Tropico Avenue	7.22
Ninth Street	7.75
Lomita Avenue	8.00
Glendale (Fourth Street)	8.39
Arden Avenue	9.50
Casa Verdugo	9.64
Bliss	9.88

MILEAGES: (Glendale to Burbank)	
Arden Avenue	9.50
Cypress Avenue	13.41
Eton Drive	15.11

FREQUENCY OF SERVICE — 1911: every 20 to 30 minutes (54 round trips daily) to Glendale; 1941: every 2 to 20 minutes (approximately 150 round trips daily, with about 50 continuing to Burbank).

RUNNING TIME — 1911: 24 minutes to San Fernando Road, 28 minutes to Lomita Avenue, 30 minutes to Broadway, 33 minutes to Arden Avenue, and 34 minutes to Casa Verdugo.

ABOVE LEFT: A Hollywood Boulevard trolley, noted for its center entrance, was en route to the Subway Terminal in 1952. ABOVE RIGHT: This scene of a trolley operating between San Bernardino and Colton was made in 1938. BELOW: These technicians were servicing the trolley wire from a motorized tower car in 1943. (All Three Photographs: Stephen D. Maguire Collection)

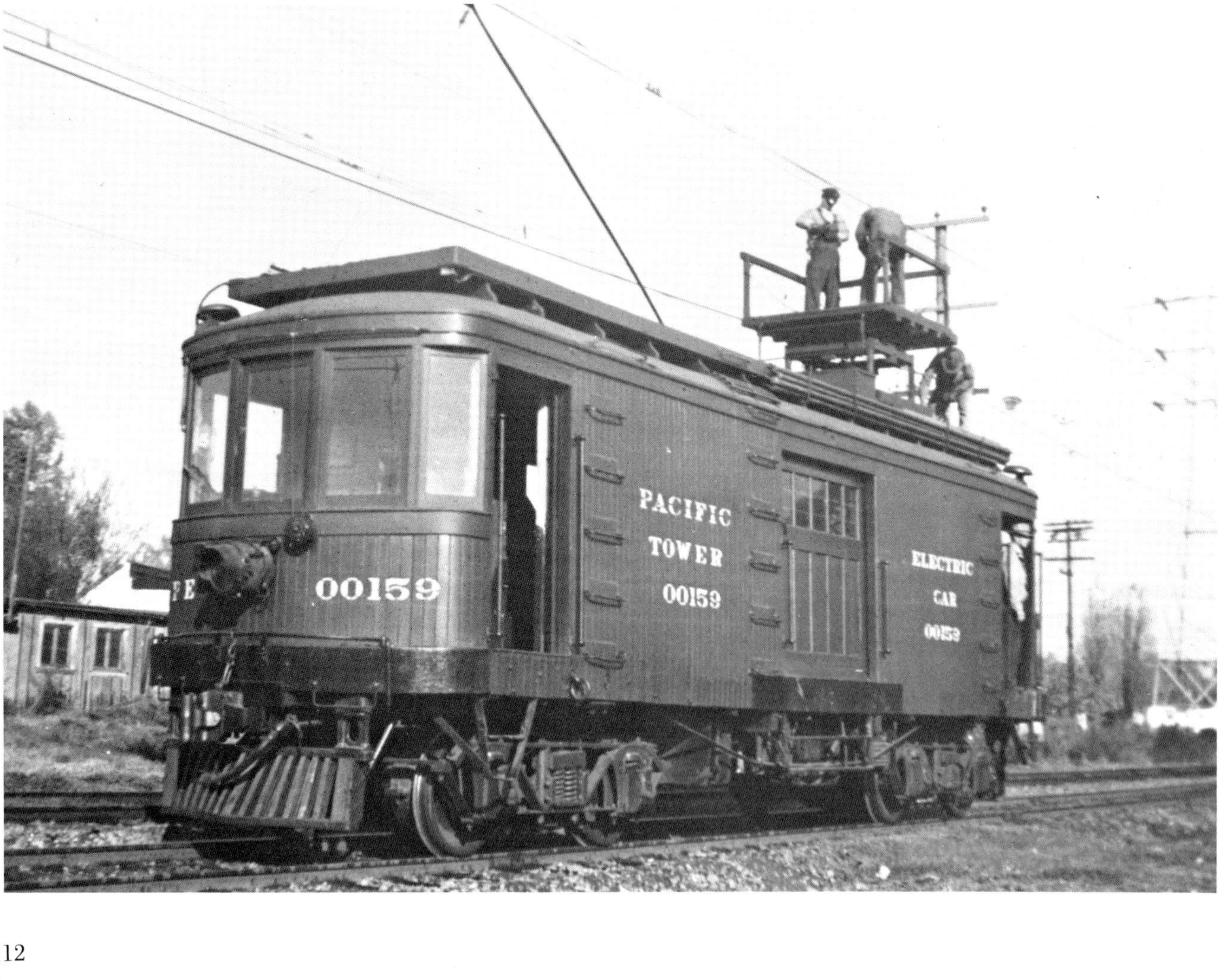